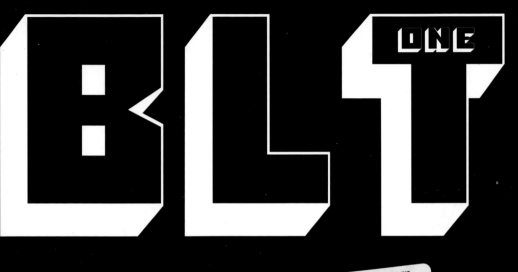

BLT ONE

KU-246-518

BANKSY LOCATIONS & TOURS · VOLUME 1

Banksy Locations (& Tours) - Vol 1
Published in the Independent Peoples' Republic of Wiltshire by shellshock publishing
Fifth Edition
Copyright © Martin Bull 2013

ISBN 978-0-9554712-5-4

Print Management by Sam @ TU Ink - **www.tuink.co.uk**

TU Ink are specialists in managing print projects for Trade Unions so I am very happy to use them for my print
needs and feel I am doing my little bit to help them continue to support Trade Unions.

INTRODUCTION

Before I released the 4th Edition of this book in 2010, I used to introduce my book by asking if the reader fancied wandering the streets of London, looking for (mainly) Banksy art and sidetracking to various quirky local attractions in parts of London they may never have visited before, or whether they prefered just sitting at home in a comfy chair (slippers and pipe optional, but highly recommended in these days of weapons of mass destruction), gazing at photos of his street work and learning about them.

Well, this unique, 100% unofficial, book is more of a history book now because lots of the art has gone since 2006, when I was the first person to publish a book about Banksy's art. The 'tours' originally showed you how to link Banksy's street work into 3 walking tours but are now pretty much redundant.

Readers who are interested can obviously still happily visit the 'active' ones (and get free updates from me as to which are still living), but please don't expect to be able to make the few remaining ones into an intensive tour anymore. Most people will now unashamedly be reading my book on the sofa or in the toilet.

Oh well, it was good whilst the tours side of the book lasted, and I still feel the book has a lot of worth because the tours and locations of 2006 - 2009 are now the pictoral archaeology of tomorrow. The bottom line is that I supply the information and the history, and you use it as you wish.

Please don't expect pseudo-intellectual ramblings in this book on what this art means, how the Banksy phenomenon took off, who he is, who he isn't, why my grandmother looks a bit like Arsene Wenger, or what the learned difference is between different types of art. I'm not that interested in intellectualising all this. A bloke creeping around in the middle of the night, getting sweaty and potentially getting nicked for painting for free on the streets, is just about the most non-intellectual state of affairs I can imagine in life.

I'll let you decide what it means to you.   Martin Bull

BLT Donations

Back in 2005, before my books existed, I met Les, a Big Issue seller, in Bristol. Chatting with him reminded me not to judge a book by its cover, and to take time to listen to people. It's something I have to remind myself of everyday though, and I still often fail.

I had always planned to use my books and related activities to generate money for commendable causes and people in need, so when I produced this book about free art on the streets, it seemed obvious to me who to raise money for; a donkey sanctuary. Only kidding.

For the first 4 editions of this book I personally donated a lot of the proceeds from sales and other various fundraising activities to The Big Issue Foundation (registered charity no. 1049077).

In all I donated £31,266.

Unfortunately I now have a young family and no money, so although I cannot afford to donate what little I may make from this latest edition, I would still like to encourage readers, if they can, to think about supporting any organisations who work to assist homeless and vulnerably housed people.

Thank you.

CONTENTS

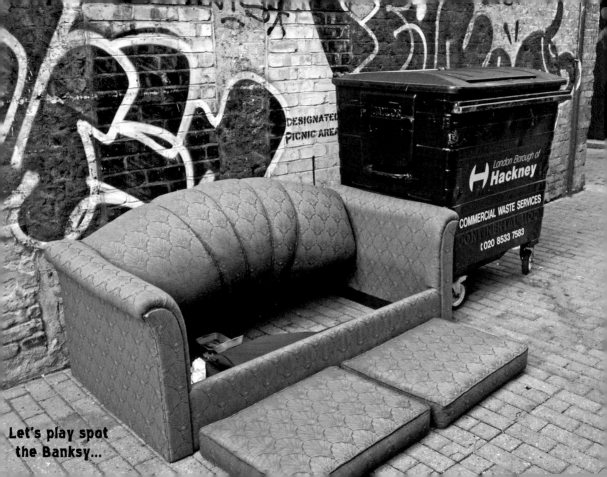

Let's play spot
the Banksy...

The Geeky Bit

Throughout 2006 many people responded to my leading questions and downright Miss Marple-esque annoyance of where to find a lot of this free art. I also discovered a lot myself whilst wandering the streets like a stray dog, following hunches and leads, and smelling the odd lamp-post to get that authentic feel. Over the next seven years I have continued to give and take information from various sources.

In an effort to share this info and to let people take their own photos (if they want to - it's not compulsory) I gave a lot of free location information on internet groups/forums/maps, and in 2006 I ran a ground breaking series of free guided tours in London, long before all these expensive tours came along to take from artists and offer nothing back. All of my efforts then accidentally formulated this book, especially the first two editions when the 'tours' were more do-able.

Although the days of 'tours' are over, some of the locations in the book still exist (as of October 2013 usually), and I will post free book/status updates on my website - www.shellshockpublishing.co.uk

I can also send these updates to you by email if you want - email me at - m@shellshockpublishing.co.uk

I will try to continue to contribute art / location information on the internet, especially on the Banksy group on flickr - www.flickr.com/groups/banksy/

BUY BYE BYE, SALE SELL SELL

(a.k.a. - leave them on the streets please)

Without wishing to sound too grave or pompous (this is graffiti / street art after all, where there aren't any rules really...), I feel that recent circumstances mean it's an apt time to give a resume of my personal feelings on removing, buying, and selling street pieces by Banksy. You of course have free will to do whatever you want to, hopefully using your conscience and internal moral compass.

First things first. This is only in regard to pieces done on the streets, and NOT canvases, screen prints, etc.

Without even knowing what others may think, my natural feeling has always clearly been to 'leave them on the street where they are supposed to be'. Simple as that. I don't need to intellectualise it by going on about the utilitarian 'gift' of work to the street, and the 'democracy of street art'. Whilst people have these inane discussions, real writers are taking risks out on train tracks and climbing shonky drainpipes.

This issue has raised its head higher for me because some people have tried to use BLT as a type of provenance when they are dealing in street pieces. For example, the door the 'Refuse Store Rat' in Clerkenwell was on (see location F8) was removed in 2007 and in Sept 2008 it turned up in a Contemporary Art auction by the Scottish auctioneer 'Lyon & Turnball'. This auction controversially contained five Banksy street pieces, all allegedly 'authenticated' by 'Vermin', a company that has no connection to Banksy.

I was very unhappy when a friend told me they had referenced this book in their description of the piece. I rattled off a complaint to Lyon & Turnball, but they refused to take out the reference to BLT. My follow up emails went unanswered (not surprisingly I guess, especially as the third one was childishly smug that their auction had been a colossal flop). Their estimate price was £20-25,000, but it remained unsold.

My books are a bit of fun really and are not meant to provide some sort of claim of provenance for a street piece. I'm simply a big geeky fan of most of Banksy's work, and these are meant as information books and DIY guides. Believe it or not these books have actually been quite hard work as well. They are not sales catalogues, nor a map to find what pieces to steal, take to auction or buy from the owner. And anyway, Banksy and Pest Control are the only people that can provide 'provenance' for anything (definitely not me), and quite correctly they will not give provenance on street pieces... because... they don't want to. Is that an accident? No, it's because street pieces are meant for the street.

This particular auction gave rise to a rare statement from Banksy, when The Evening Standard quoted him as writing: "Graffiti art has a hard enough life as it is - with council workers wanting to remove it and kids wanting to draw moustaches on it, before you add hedgefund managers wanting to chop it out and hang it over the fireplace. For the sake of keeping all street art where it belongs *I'd encourage people not to buy anything by anybody unless it was created for sale in the first place*". (my italics)

Similarly, Pest Control added a note of warning about buying street pieces, when it wrote on its web site in 2010: " 'Banksy' would encourage anyone wanting to purchase one of his images to do so with extreme caution, but does point out that many copies are superior in quality to the originals. Since the creation of Pest Control in January 2008 we have identified 89 street pieces... falsely attributed to the artist."

The most informative internet piece on this thorny subject can still (October 2013) be found at -
http://www.standard.co.uk/news/banksys-dont-bank-on-it-6813264.html

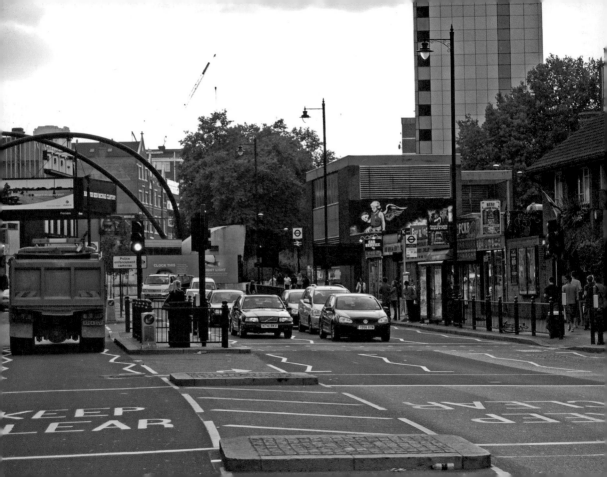

Hoxton Shoreditch

This was the biggest of the three tours by far, and at a pretty decent pace it took us three hours. It could have been far more if I included all the streets and back alleys.

This is the capital of UK street art - Hoxton, Old Street, Shoreditch, Brick Lane - the creative, yet run-down, neuvo trendy East End. The streets (and railway bridges and skanky alleys) are literally awash with sprayed art of different styles, plus paste-ups, stickers, installations, art projects and all sorts of weird and wonderful dribbling creative juices: picture frames on the street; nailed up art; tattooists; photographers; fashion victims, and maybe even Nathan Barley on his poxy BMX if you are unlucky enough.

The local Council are a lot less tolerant now, but fortunately the walls are speedily changing anyway, and private walls now abound, so even though most of the featured art has now gone, you're bound to always find something new in this area or even something old that had somehow passed you by.

Literally stumbling across 'the maid' (see S20) early-ish one Sunday morning in May 2006 (I suspect Banksy did it in the small hours of that morning and that I was one of the first people to ever see it sober) is a pleasure you can only really get by wandering around, keeping your eyes open, and following your destiny. You will be startled by how many random moments have led me to come across this free art.

So I suggest getting out of the house and taking the dog for a walk in the area, or borrowing a dog if you don't have one.

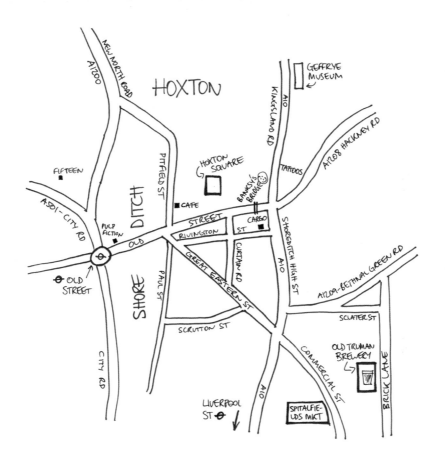

poison rat

Bits of this rat, and the green waste, can still just be made out on the wall of Oliver's Yard, by City Road - A501 (Post Code - EC1Y 1AU Map/GPS reference - TQ 32796 82288), but it's fairer to conclude that this rat has now passed away and gone to rat paradise.

It had been there since at least mid 2005, and had been used in the Banksy books and on his website.

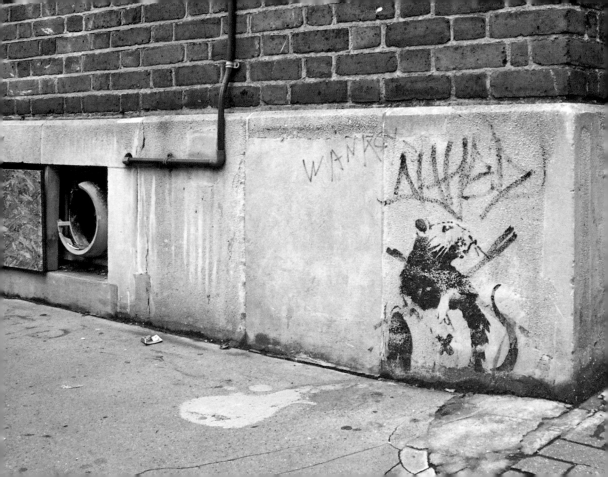

check out the wall...

This long, slightly secluded, wall, is located by Exit 8 of Old Street tube station, and used to be an ever changing open air art gallery.

The artist Arofish was probably the first to paint this wall white one day and then come back later to add his 'Holy War' piece to it. He used the old trick of posing as a workman. It's amazing what you can get away with in life when you have a £2.99 hi-viz jacket and overalls on, and a bit of a swagger.

After that it had a succession of art and paint overs, including this cheeky reference by El Chivo to the frequent repainting.

However it's mainly been blank since 2007 as the clampdown on nice walls like this one has progressed through the area.

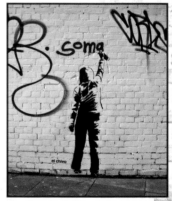

Soma by El Chivo, in June 2006, followed by 'paint it black...paint it white...' by El Chivo, October 2006 (both soon painted over)

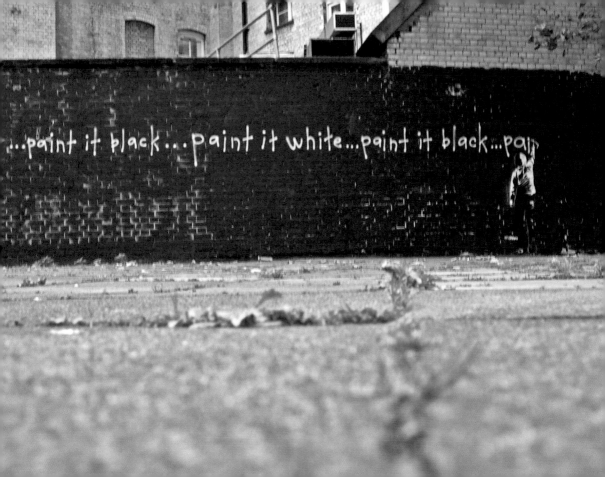

microphone rat

This used to live on an old disused entrance to Moorfields Eye Hospital on City Road (by Cayton Street - Post Code - EC1V 9EH. Map/GPS reference - TQ 32551 82701)

It was a great example of a large microphone rat. I like to imagine it belting out 'My Way' on a karaoke machine or maybe toasting at a sweaty sound system clash in Kingston (Jamaica, not Upon-Thames).

It dwelt there since at least mid 2004. For half of 2006 it was covered up during renovations to the building, but it managed to survive. It was released again in October 2006 and endured nicely until early December 2007 when a gert big bit of wood was plonked over it. The wood was weakly screwed over it and the rat could still be seen under the wood for several years until the Hospital decided to auction if off on 7th October 2010. It raised Ł30,000 for research into new treatment for eye disease.

The Evening Standard reported that "Banksy and his team were involved throughout the planning and had helped the Moorfield to cut the picture... from the wall" and that it appeared to be the man himself who made last minute restorations to the work just before the auction.

There was the obligatory tinge of irony to the auction though. Jeffrey Archer was the 'celebrity' auctioneer and it was held in the Saatchi Gallery. Banksy had famously remarked in an ultra rare face-to-face interview with The Guardian in 2003, that "I wouldn't sell s**t to Charles Saatchi. If I sell 55,000 books and however many screen prints, I don't need one man to tell me I'm an artist... No, I'd never sell anything to him." And in what seems to be another reference to the wife throttler, Mr.B also told artnet in 2003 that, "I don't like the gallery system. These days the value of art seems to come down to whether one millionaire likes it or not."

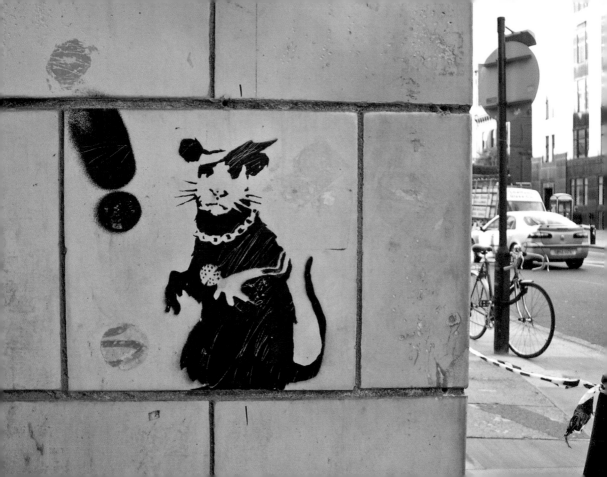

cutting rats & gangsta rat

The cutting rats on the right used to be outside Fifteen Restaurant, on Westland Place (Post Code - N1 7LP. Map/GPS reference - TQ 32551 82807).

Being an advocate for tree hugging pinko liberals this stencil was done next to Jamie Oliver's 'social restaurant' Fifteen in oh so trendy Hoxton, as if some rats were breaking in. Mr.B also used the same stencil on the gates to the Greenpeace office in London (see BLT Vol 2). Is there no end to this man's humour? ☺

They had dwelt there since at least mid 2004, but they disappeared circa March 2007. The rats were actually on pains of blackened glass, which were removed & replaced, presumably by the owners of the building.

A gangsta rat lived just around the corner from at least 2005 but was whitewashed in 2006; well before the cutting rats went. The inset photo is the best photo I have of it I'm afraid, as it had been buffed by the time I went back to take onefrom a better angle.

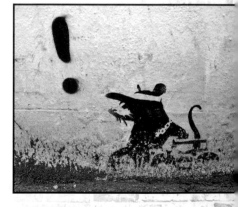

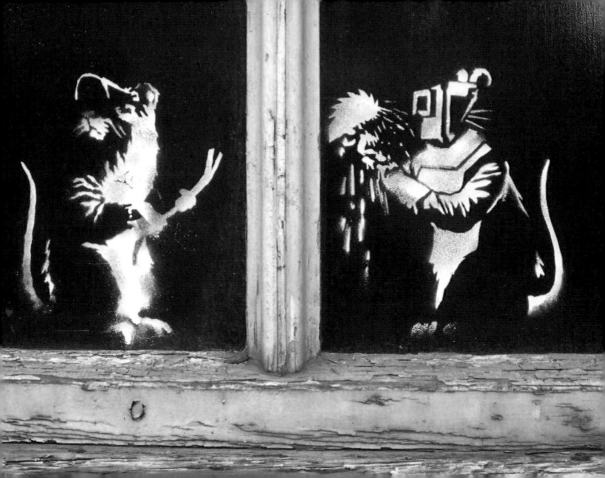

smiley copper

This used to be on the slightly tucked away wall at the corner of Vestry Street and East Road (Post Code - N1 7LP. Map/GPS reference - TQ 32551 82807).

My photo shows the 'Smiley' Copper on the badly peeling wall, after having been amended by an artist unknown to make it a rather unique 'blank faced' copper instead. Also rather uniquely a large Banksy tag covered the stomach area.

This exact graffiti is shown in Banksy's book 'Wall & Piece', and has also been on his web site, where it was used to introduce the idea of 'Clubism'; a tongue-in-cheek new movement in art described as, "...dirty and mindless but it's the best way to get over a bad week at work".

It had lived there since at least spring 2004 (and possibly a lot earlier than that) but was incompetently buffed in February 2007.

Shepard Fairey later added a pasteup to the wall during his November 2007 visit to London (see inset photo right).

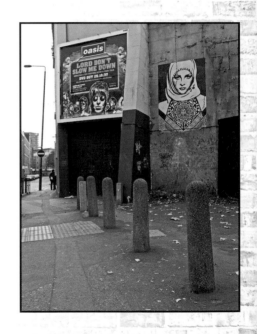

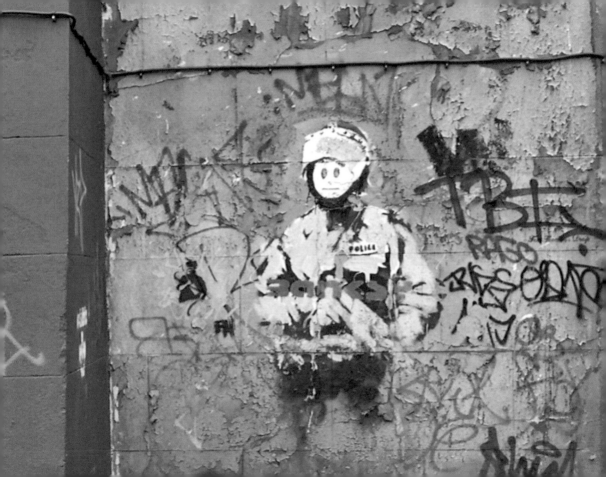

girl with balloon

This was on the side of some flats on the New North Road (A1200), close to Wimbourne Street (Post Code - N1 6TA. Map/GPS reference - TQ 32696 83342) and had been shown on Banksy's website many years ago.

Sometime around Spring 2006 the red balloon was repainted, by a person unknown. The whole piece was later painted over in March 2007, but for a while it could still just be seen through the new grey paint. I suspected this might happen as the local housing estate was being renovated and when that happens they generally give everything that doesn't move a coat of paint as well.

Although this was the last Girl With Balloon to survive in London, they used to be surprisingly abundant. Three versions existed on the South Bank. One was on the east side of Waterloo Bridge and was featured in 'Wall and Piece'. Others existed on Clink Street, and on the east side of Blackfriars Bridge. That one featured in Woody Allen's dreadful film 'Match Point'. Another trio were clustered around Shoreditch (one on Paul Street, one on the corner of Pitfield Street and Bowling Green Walk, and one on Provost Street), and finally there was a lone one in Clerkenwell on St.John Street.

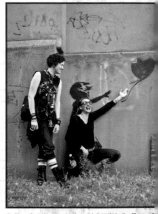

This image is consistently choosen by fans (especially females) as their favourite image, and its meaning is endlessly debated on dull forums. Is the girl grabbing for the balloon (lost love?) or is she letting love go? Who cares! LOL. I would have thought it was relatively clear, as his books furnish the following explanation, "When the time comes to leave, just walk away quietly and don't make any fuss". When Pictures On Walls (POW) used to sell the image as a print, the description read, "Banksy was never his mother's favourite - and he was an only child".

Erika & Nhatt at the Girl With Balloon in 2006

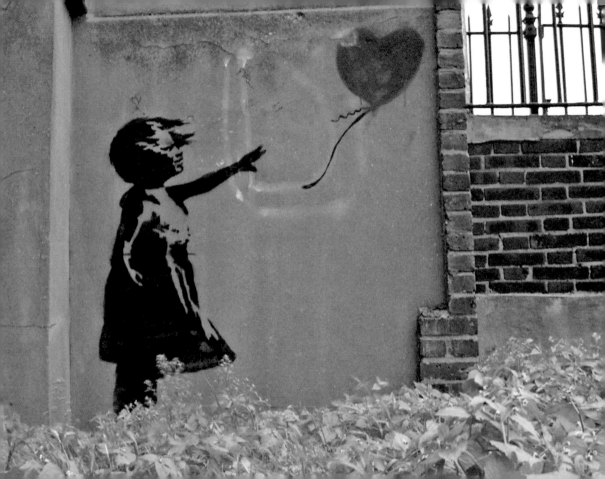

canal hoodie

This existed from at least early 2005 under the foot bridge that goes over the Regent's Canal. The bridge is the pedestrianised section of road between Shepherdess Walk and Packington Square (Post Code - N1 7JL. Map/GPS reference - TQ 32282 83375).

In late May 2010 it was totally blacked out though, and replaced by the following comment - 'I see a Banksy and have got to paint it black - Team Robbo rollin with the Stones' - alongside a burlesque of John Pasche's famous Rolling Stones mouth logo. This was presumably part of the longer-term fallout from the now infamous 'Robbo' incident in 2009 (in a nut shell Banksy amended/went over an ancient piece by veteran writer Robbo further along the Regent's Canal in Camden, and all hell broke loose afterwards).

It was a good example of how Banksy must re-use stencils, as it seems identical to the 'Tourist Information' image. One of these was just off the Hackney Road in Ion Square and another version had been camped in Hoxton Square circa 2004. The inset photo shows the Hackney version. It had almost gone by the time I found it in 2006.

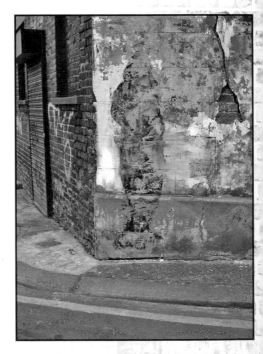

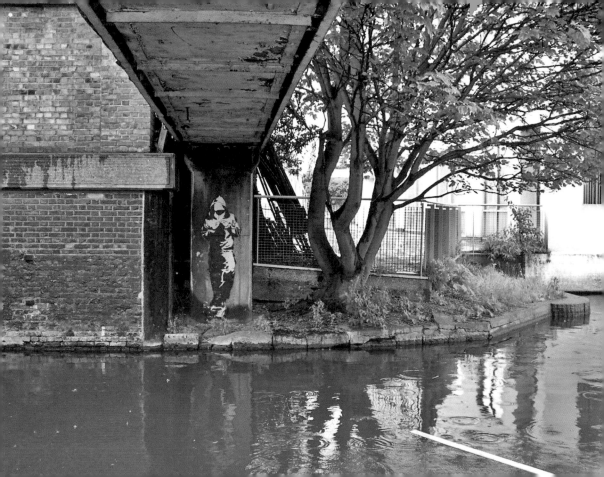

umbrella rat

A splendid little umbrella rat used to reside in the corner of a large whitewashed section of wall next to the newsagents on the corner of East Road and New North Road (Post Code - N1 6JB. Map/GPS reference - TQ 32877 83049).

Before the wall was whitewashed I think there was a myriad of other art there (by other writers / artists), but only the Banksy was spared.

Six months later though the whole wall was painted over.

I'll always remember a nice moment on my second free Banksy tour in Shoreditch when I was outside this building, giving the throng of over 50 people fragments of history about it. A rather hippie-fied resident of the building opened the door in his dressing gown (it was about 2pm by this point), and was slightly bemused at a huge group of people goggling at his mainly blank Victorian wall.

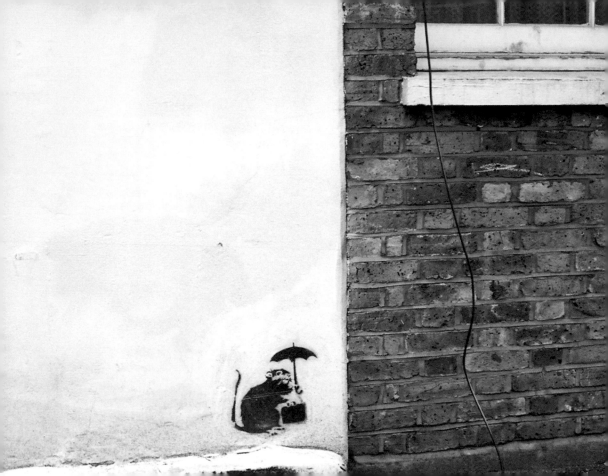

umbrella rat

This was on the metal newsagents box of City Supermarket, 57 Pitfield Street - near Haberdasher Street (Post Code - N1 6BU. Map/GPS reference - TQ 33014 82852).

A pretty awful specimen, with loads of runs (and therefore maybe a fake), but it was a good example of how these metal newsagent boxes are a great target for artists and sticker merchants because they are left out all night for secure milk and newspaper deliveries.

This was buffed, circa December 2006.

BLT TIP

I don't eat animal products so I can't judge the kebabs for you, but the 'Best Kebab & Café' at the bottom of Pitfield Street is a good down-to-earth place.

It does a lovely falafel meal, and the coffee is great too.

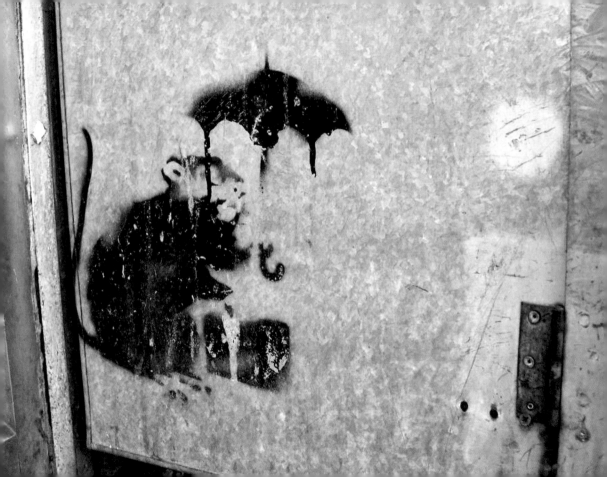

'have a nice day' (happy chopper)

Post Code - EC2A 3JD
Map/GPS reference - TQ 32978 82519

Location & Daring Tales of Climbing on Roofs (hardly)

Above the now empty 'Wa Do Chinese Fast Food' shop on the corner of Old Street and Tabernacle Street. A very large Banksy tag with an exclamation mark (something he only did on earlier pieces) is out of shot, to the right.

There is a great photo of this in the snow in Banksy's 'Wall and Piece' book, when the shop below used to be 'Franco's Fish & Chips'. It dates the piece to 2003.

Not long after it was done it was partly obscured by a massive advertising hoarding above it, in addition to the existing shop sign below it.

But you could climb up on the roof to get a better look at it. Loads of painting paraphernalia is up there. Maybe some of it was used to do the piece?

The image is very similar to the rare A2 sized poster given away with some copies of the March 2003 issue of the magazine 'Sleazenation'.

Status

Still there (October 2013), but very obscured and has been mainly covered in transparent plastic since Spring 2010. It can be easier to look at from a distance, or from buildings opposite if you can wangle your way in.

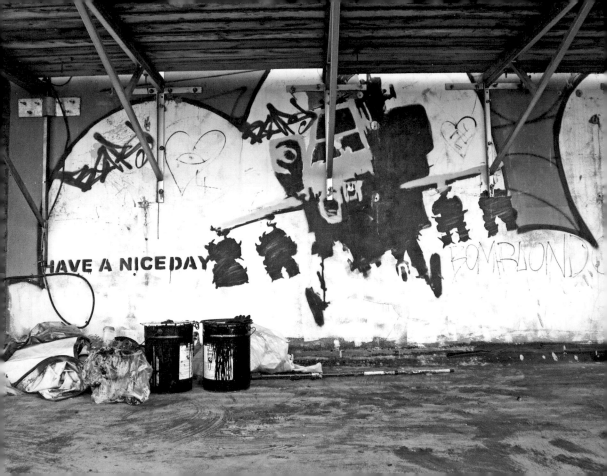

S11

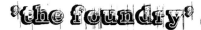
"the foundry" (or whatever it's new name will be)

Post Code - EC2A 3JL   **Map/GPS reference - TQ 33057 82557**

Location, Some History & A Bit Of A Rant

The inside of this eclectic bar/exhibition area (co-founded by the great Bill Drummond), situated where Old Street and Great Eastern Street collide, had a chaotic smorgansbord of art on the walls downstairs, by the toilets (and inside them - I did also check out the Ladies, but only in the name of research of course). Any artist who had had work displayed in the venue, or was generally considered good enough, was 'allowed' to add to the wall.

Banksy contributed a grin reaper, a happy chopper, and a tag.

Notable others on the wall include Arofish, who had an exhibition there in the mid 2000's, and the Faile collective.

Although a voluntary group has been allowed to run the building in a lovely collective style in the interim, several years ago the owners, Park Plaza Hotels, were given permission to knock down most of the site (which includes location S13 - which is supposed to be saved) and build an 18 storey 'art hotel' on it. Oh the irony of building an 'art hotel' on the vestiges of a genuinely creative venue!

Status

As this edition went to press (October 2013), this section of the building was due to reopen as a sort of modern day soup kitchen. I've been assured that the Banksy's still exist on the wall downstairs but I'm not sure if the toilets will be opened to punters.

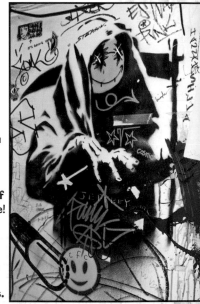

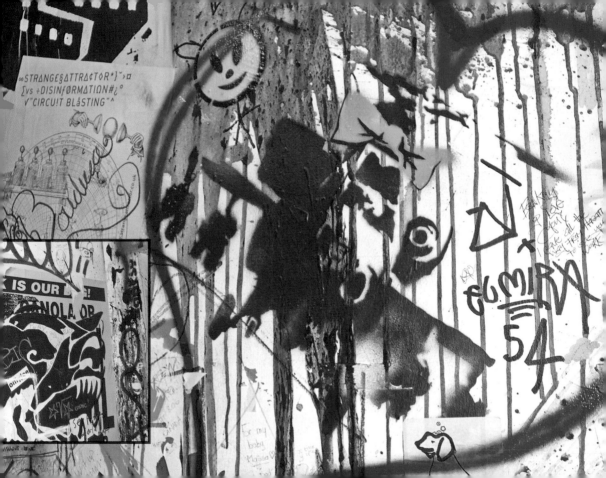

the 'pulp fiction' site

This is probably the most famous site regularly used by Banksy, but it was also notoriously hard to photograph and view. Staying further away often gives you a better view of it. It's above a row of shops on Old Street, near Vine Street (Post Code - EC1V 9PB. Map/GPS reference - TQ 32834 82543).

From 2003 to 2005 it had Banksy's famous 'Pulp Fiction' piece on it. That endured until just after the 7th July bombings in 2005 when a blunt message to '**** Al Qaida' completely covered it.

In May 2006 Shepard Fairey put a massive Andre the Giant paster up, and Faile flanked it on both sides with their snarling dog wheat pastes (see right). 'Banksy was ere' was then crudely added on top in a pink paint that looked suspiciously the same shade that both faile and Banksy had recently used around town (see Location F5, and the BLT Tip between F8 & F9, plus several in BLT Vol 2). 'TDO' (Take Down Oker) was also painted on it, so maybe it was something involving that?

In early July 2006 a new version of Pulp Fiction went up, this time with Jackson & Travolta dressed as bananas & holding guns, rather than the other way around, as the original showed them. This was followed in September with a complete paste over, and then a crudely drawn message that 'Nothing Lasts Forever'. See photos overleaf. As they say, great art is all in the compositio...

Throughout the rest of 2006 and most of 2007 the wall was pretty rubbish. Everytime I went to the area I always checked it out, and every time I was disappointed. I almost stopped bothering.

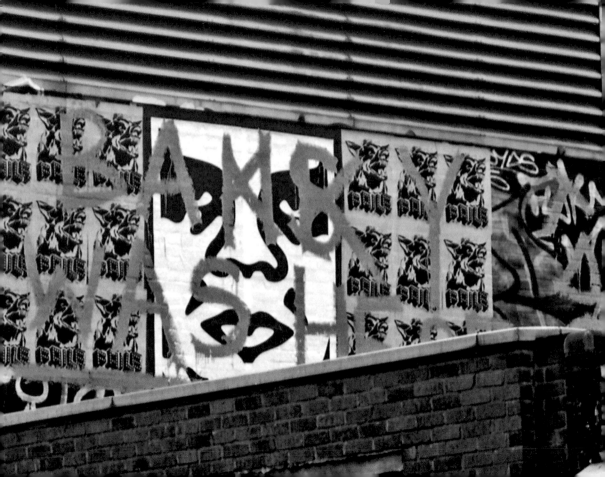

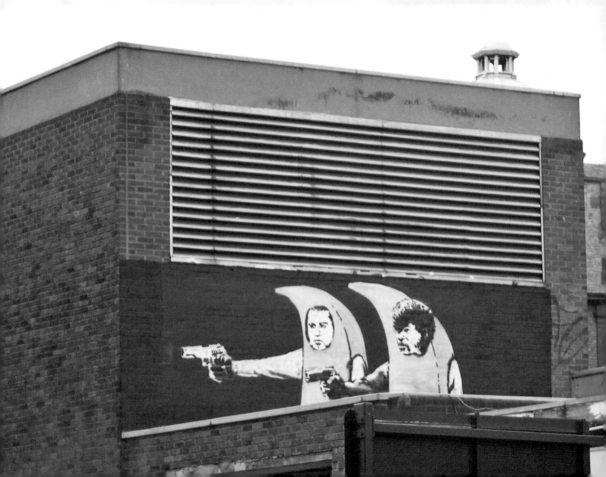

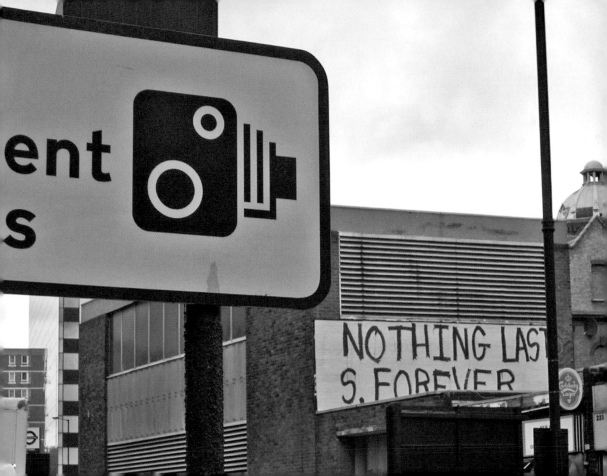

Fast forward. It's 5.30pm on 9th September 2007. I'm on the top deck (the best seat in the house for art and graf spotting) as my bus goes past the site. I half heartedly turn to look at the wall. OMG! I jump up, ring the buzzer, and stop the bus. I'm excited not just because it's new, but because it has Banksy metaphorically written all over it (although many amazingly doubted it at first). Most importantly it was the first piece of street art for months to actual stop me in my tracks, to move me, & to make me fall in love again. The quality was amazing, and the subject poignant. For me, Banksy was back on top and the high class work was saying 'I'm the daddy'.

Interestingly it was noticed that at 3pm that day the site was still shrouded in blue tarpaulin, some of which was later left on the roof. This was becoming a favourite Banksy trick; to wholely cover a site in tarpaulin/scaffolding, to gain the time and privacy to do a top job.

Soon it was on Banksy's website, with an explanation. It was called 'Old St Cherub' and was done shortly after several children had suffered the consequences of gun crime. Banksy wrote "Last time I hit this spot I painted a crap picture of two men in banana costumes waving handguns. A few weeks later a writer called Ozone completely dogged it and then wrote 'If it's better next time I'll leave it' in the bottom corner. When we lost Ozone (Ozone - 21 year old Bradley Chapman - was killed by a train in January 2007) we lost a fearless graffiti writer and as it turns out a pretty perceptive art critic. Ozone - Rest In Peace".

In late February 2009 it was dogged by the prolific writer 10 foot, with the message 'Say No To Art Fags. R.I.P. Ozone'. The same message appeared over another Banksy work (see Location EL12 in BLT Vol 2).

The wall was blackwashed in mid March, and in late June 2009, the artist 'Mantis' took the space for his personal take on people with bananas and the lack of attention that Africa gets. The wall has rarely been used in the last few years, which is a shame, but is merely more evidence that 'street artists' using the area have been less and less bold as time goes by, and are more 'artists' than 'street'. No-one wants to get sweaty these days.

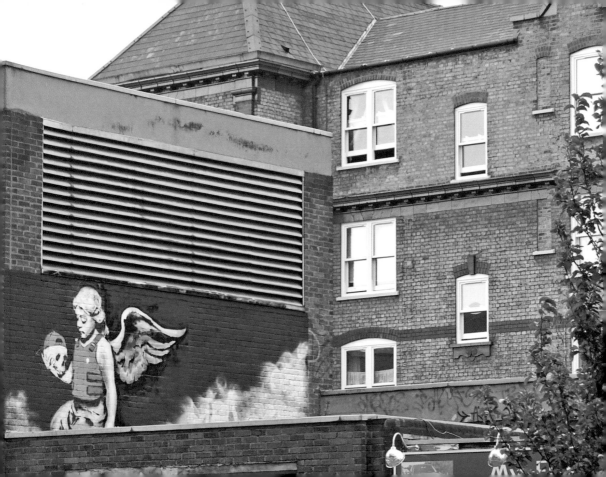

TV out of the window & a giant rat

These are technically still there, in the old car park (called 'Ridgeway Place') on the corner of Rivington Street and Old Street/Great Eastern Street (Post Code - EC2A 3DT. Map/GPS reference - TQ 33059 82549).

The wall has loads of art on it, including Banksy's TV out of the Window (which was featured in 'Wall and Piece' next to the 'Broken Window Theory' info, and dates it to 2004), and an enormous rat with a knife and fork. The later is the same size and shape as the rat done in Liverpool for the 2004 Art Biennial - see BLT Vol 2 for full details.

Both have been there since 2004, and over the following years an influx of other art got closer and closer to them. In December 2007 they were covered in wooden hoardings, apparently in readiness for them to be removed and sold. That never happened. The hoarding was soon covered with art, mainly from the Burning Candy crew (see inset photo on the next double page) but the Banksy's are still definately there, underneath the wood (October 2013).

It's potential future seems rather uncertain though. As mentioned a few pages ago, planning permission has been given to knock down the entire site (which includes Location S11) and build a 18 storey, 350 room, 'art hotel' on it. I love the paradox of an 'art hotel', because Banksy, Elmo, faile, Eine, Arofish, Roa & all the others dotted around the building aren't REAL artists of course!

However, Hackney Council have stipulated that THIS WALL must be 'saved'. Hmm, it might be interesting to see how that is executed. The Islington Tribune reported Banksy's pithy reaction to be, "It's a bit like demolishing the Tate and preserving the ice cream van out the front".

The 'TV out of the Window' image was first seen as part of a Blur photo shoot on 24th August 2003 for the launch issue of the Observer Music Monthly in Sept 2003. Farm buildings in Yorkshire were used as the backdrop for the photos, and the front cover shows Blur standing in

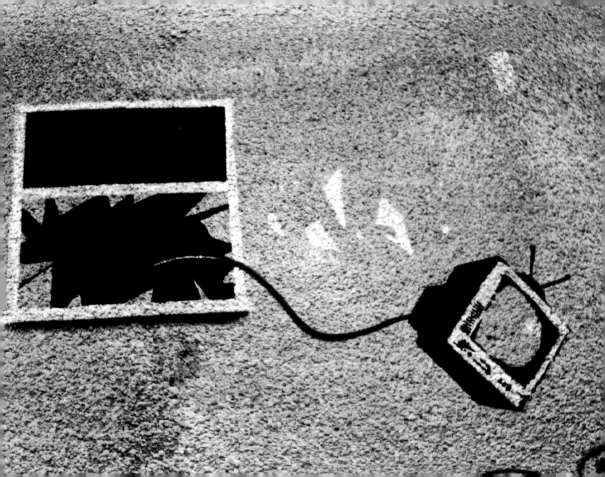

front of the 'TV' artwork (Banksy is reported to be "standing just out of shot"). It was originally supposed to be done at the Leeds Festival (where Blur headlined), but there were no walls there. And the whole thing almost fell through when, as the magazine stated, "two days before the shoot, Banksy went AWOL. It later transpired that he had been arrested in Berlin for defacing a building". So, out in the countryside they knocked on the door of Norwood House farm, and the rest is history.

In June 2008, the farm owner, Stephen Walmesley, put it up for auction with an estimated value of ₤30,000-₤50,000. It failed to sell, and probably wasn't helped by the piece being on thick concrete blocks and measuring over 2 metres high. The funniest part is how he decided to try to sell it. The art specialist who organised it is quoted as saying that "Another client of mine is a pig farmer and is interested in Banksy. He casually mentioned that one of his pals had one on

his barn wall". Things seem to have massively changed in the pastoral regions recently. Anyone for farm art?

Banksy did two others on the farm. One was a girl hugging a TV (which was sold at auction in 2007 for ₤38,400), and the third is believed to be a practise piece on a bit of gate.

There used to be another 'TV' in Angel (Islington). It was on the side of an old building (since demolished) near the junction of the A1 and A501.

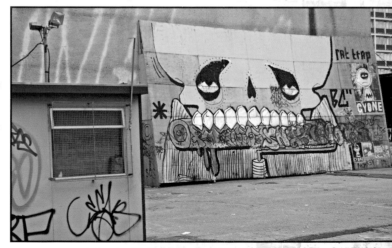

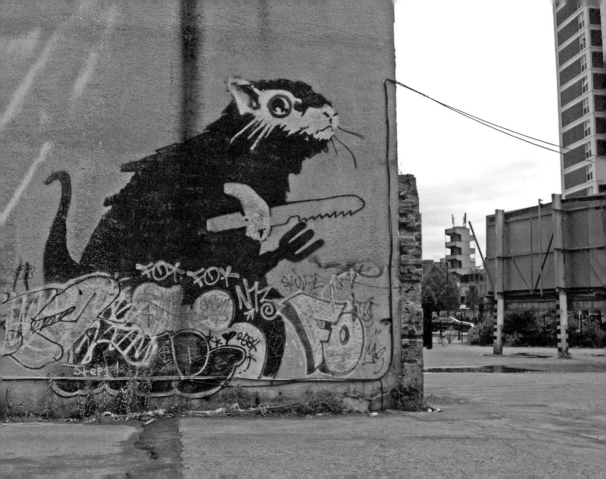

grin reaper

The reapers scythe can still just be made out on the side of a bar called 'Yard' (Post Code - **EC2A 4N. Map/GPS** reference - **TQ 33003 82467**), on the corner of Paul Street and Tabernacle Street, but it's easier and fairer to consider this to be a gonner.

Well, it has been there since 2003, so it has paid its dues.

Overall it was never hardly worth mentioning, but it is an effective example of something that fades away, or is buffed to within an inch of its life.

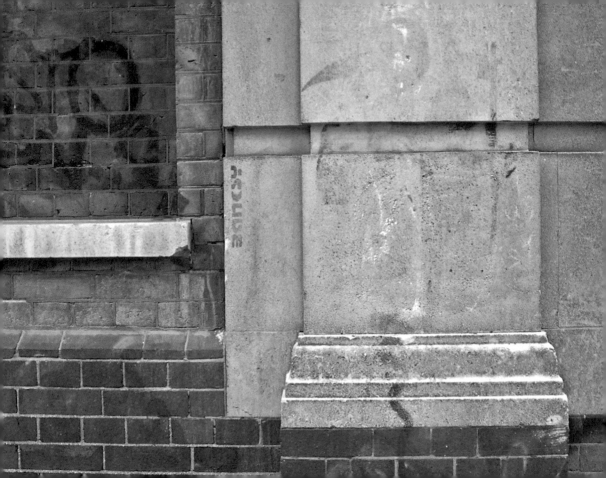

grin reaper

This stunning yellow grin reaper used to hover on a striking blue wall where the old Pictures On Walls office was located on Scrutton Street (Post Code - EC2A 4RT. Map/GPS reference - TQ 33030 82209).

It was tagged below it (out of shot).

This exact piece is shown in 'Wall and Piece', which dates it to 2004, and it has also been on Mr.B's website.

The magazine 'Design Week' also used it on their front cover on 11th March 2004, for an article called 'Peace Talks - A Visual Take on Conflict'.

Over the years it got dogged quite a lot, and the tag got blanked out, but it survived in some shape or form until May/June 2010 when the whole wall was 'blue-washed'.

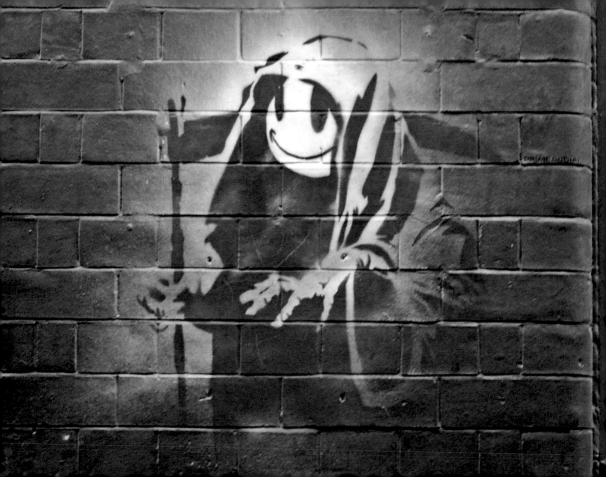

happy choppers

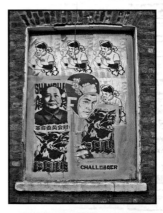

This used to be tucked away behind a blind corner on Holywell Row (Post Code - EC2A 4XB. Map/GPS reference - TQ 33113 82180), until it was mainly painted over in January 2007. The top of one helicopter was still visible for a while but when I visited again in September 2007 the whole alley was now completely blocked off and being repainted.

There regularly used to be faile paste ups on the building opposite (see top inset photo), but not anymore. It was a sort of unofficial faile history site that they pasted on every time they came over to London.

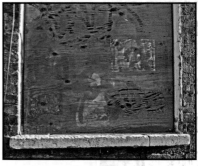

After all the faile posters went a white gangsta rat could then be seen (see bottom inset photo). This was most probably a fake. I've only ever seen one rat coloured white before (although that one was most probably real). And it seems as if this wasn't underneath the old paste-ups. If it was added after the paste-ups, then it's nearly definately fake because Banksy hasn't done small lone rats in the UK since the mid 2000's.

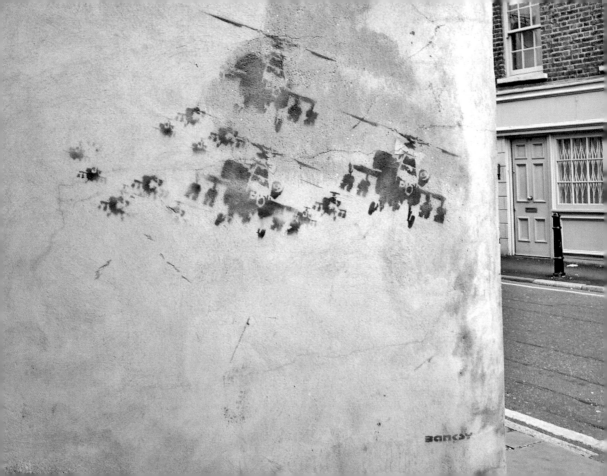

red carpet rats

This was on the corner of **Curtain Road and Christina Street**, opposite Pizza Express, and dated from at least 2004 (Post Code - **EC2A 3PT**. Map/GPS reference - **TQ 33259 82286**).

I first photographed this in January 2006 and by the time I went back a week or so later it had pretty much gone. I often revisit sites, although on this occasion I was returning principally because I had stupidly lost all my digital photos from the January visit. Doh! So for this book I've had to dig out an old black & white 35mm film photo I have of it.

For some time after the rats were just noticeable, and the red 'carpet' was still quite visible on the pavement (see inset photo - it is still visible in October 2013). Eventually more buffing meant the vermin were finally exterminated.

For several years impressive mural collabs filled the long wall behind. The last mural painted on there incorporated an RIP piece to Beastie Boy Adam 'MCA' Yauch and a tribute to influential comic and science fiction illustrator Jean 'Mœbius' Giraud, both painted by Jim Vision of End Of The Line. The building is now empty and the epic mural currently (October 2013) remains in the same pristine condition as when it was painted in May 2012.

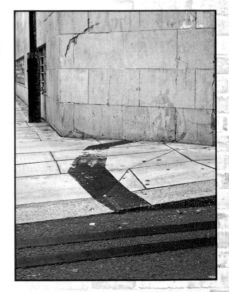

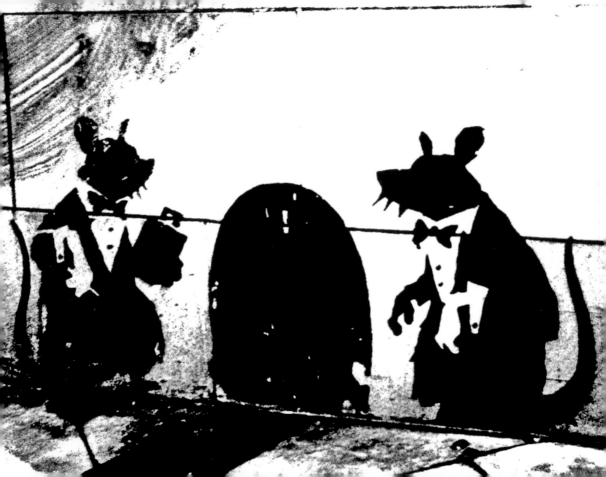

BLT TIP

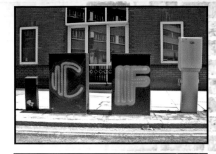

This area used to be awash with art but since 2008 there has definately been a change of attitude from the local council (Hackney). It's still well worth a wander, but in general the buffing squad, and the East London train line extension, has reduced the amount of true 'street' art. The number of private/legal walls has developed though.

The main photo shows my second Shoreditch/Hoxton tour in the New Yard Inn area, at the blind spots around the side & back of 'The Old Blue Last' pub. Banksy's 'girl with balloon' and a soldier painting an anarchy sign had been just around the corner. They went many years ago of course but these walls are still very active (October 2013) and well worth a visit.

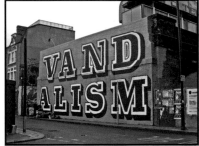

In this area Eine unleashed his new 'neon style' alphabet letters in June 2006 (see top inset photo). I think this is the best font Ben has done, and I liked it so much I bought a sweet canvas of it.

In late June 2007 he blew people away with his largest piece yet; the word 'Vandalism' on the massive back wall of the Village Underground, on Holywell Lane. It's easy to forget now that large pieces like this simply didn't use to exist & that the proclivity for larger walls has grown a lot.

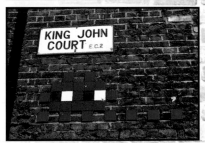

An unusually large Space Invader used to exist in the distance, on the old rail bridge (see bottom inset photo), but that Victorian brick bridge was demolished in summer 2007, to make way for a new concrete one.

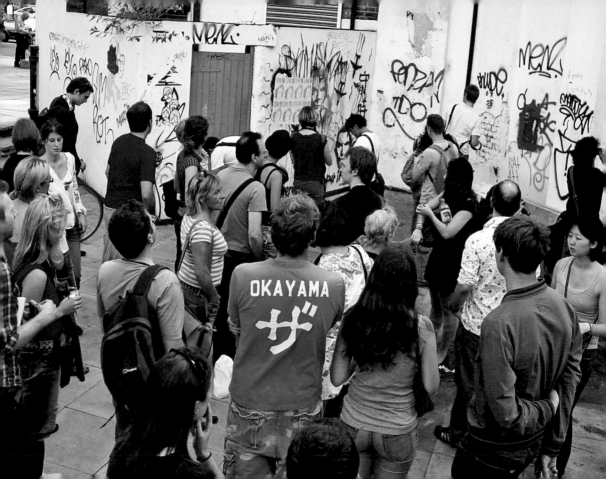

designated picnic areas

Two enigmatic 'Designated Picnic Area' stencils previously lived within a few metres of each other on Curtain Road (Post Code - EC2A 3AH. Map/GPS reference - TQ 33294 82478). Both had been there since at least autumn 2003.

1) On the small steps of a building on Curtain Road (near Curtain Place) - see the main photo.

This was one of my favourites anywhere, as the entrance it was on used to be plastered with old posters and litter, and was definitely not a place to have a picnic.

In mid 2008 fresh, bright white, doors were added to the entrance of the grubby edifice, making it look a totally incongruous mix of skanky and new. The whole building was later given the clean and tidy treatment, and in 2009 the stencil was finally gone, as it became a posh Estate Agent (Nelson's); the same way that many things have gone in Hoxton.

2) On the Curtain Road end of a soiled alley (Dereham Place). My inset photo was taken not long before it was buffed in December 2006.

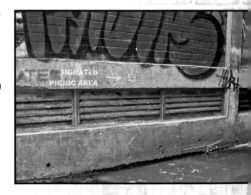

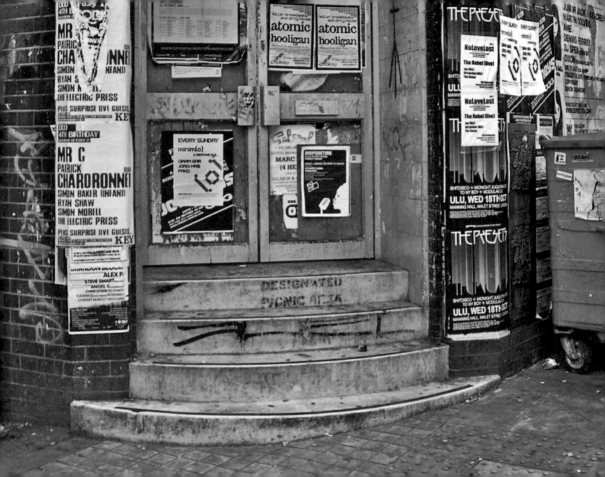

snorting copper & white line

The infamous snorting copper was just off **Curtain Road**, outside what is now called the 'Far Rockaway' bar (Post Code - **EC2A 3BS**. Map/GPS reference - **TQ 33249 82500**).

Part of the white line can still be seen (October 2013) going along the alley (Mills Court) and into a drain on Charlotte Road.

One day in May 2006 the Council came along and ineptly jet washed it. It then looked far worse (see inset photo). At least this art had been making an attempt to brighten up the streets and get our brains thinking.

It was partly shown in Banksy's best selling book 'Wall and Piece', which dates it to 2005. The book mixes and matches photos of this whiteline with the **Snorting Copper** that in reality existed by **Waterloo Train Station** (see location R6).

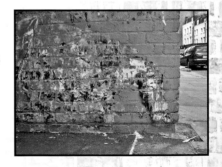

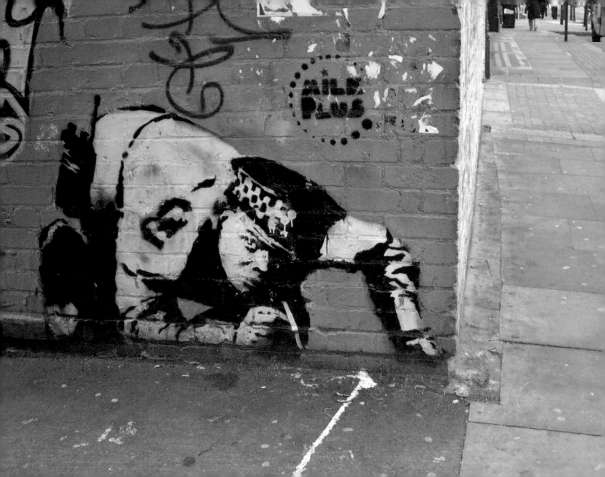

sweeping it under the carpet - "hoxton maid"

This was on the Rufus Street side of Jay Joplin's White Cube gallery in Hoxton Square (Post Code - EC2A 3PT. Map/GPS reference - TQ 33259 82286) for about 6 weeks in mid 2006 before they doubtless decided it was too much competition for their own exhibits and painted over it.

A slightly different version also appeared in Camden (see BLT Vol 2).

The special (RED) edition of The Independent newspaper on 16th May 2006 reported that, "Banksy said yesterday that the...piece was...about the democratisation of subjects in works of art. "In the bad old days, it was only popes and princes who had the money to pay for their portraits to be painted," he said. "This is a portrait of a maid called Leanne who cleaned my room in a Los Angeles motel. She was quite a feisty lady" ".

Both versions were based on the original street version he did in Los Angeles in March 2006, just before the infamous 'Barely Legal' exhibition (which incidentally had a canvas version of it on display). A drawing of the image also featured on his web site for a while, as did a photo of it on the street.

Literally being the first sober person to 'discover' this by stumbling across it early-ish one Sunday morning in May 2006 (I suspect Banksy did it in the small wee hours of that Sunday morning, the 14th) is a pleasure you can only really experience by wandering around, keeping your eyes open, and following your destiny. I'm always amazed at how many totally random situations have led me to come across some brilliant free art.

One sniffy and elitist comment about this book was that it made it too easy to find the art and therefore made it a common and accessible experience. Apparently finding things by wandering / randomness is called serendipity. I had to look that up in the dictionary ☺

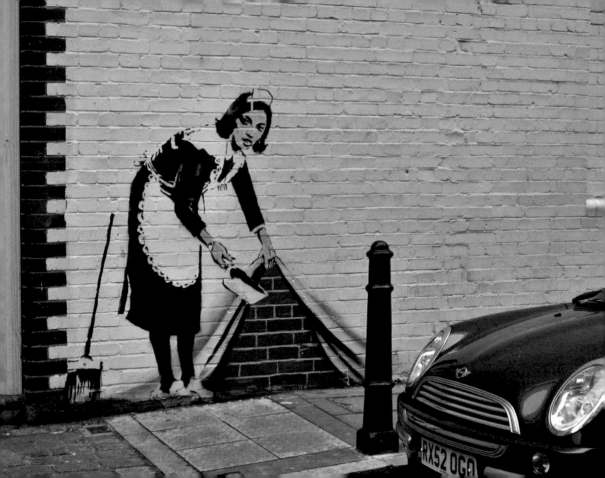

abandon hope

Another very iconic Banksy spot.

From 2002 Banksy regularly added pasted up images and messages to the train bridge across Old Street, near Shoreditch High Street, when it was dis-used (Post Code - EC1V 9LP. Map/GPS reference - TQ 33371 82674). Slogans included 'It's a Free Country', 'Wrong War', and 'We Will Win' - painted by a rat. The road is a main route to Hackney, or the City.

The final message was 'Abandon Hope - 9am to 5pm' in early April 2006, which only lasted a week or so. This was one of only a few times that Banksy used pasted up posters rather than sprayed stencils, and apparently he was close to getting caught when doing it. Film of it going up was briefly included in his film 'Exit Through the Gift Shop'.

Please excuse the poor quality photo of this one (and a few others in the book). When I started photographing art and graffiti I never dreamt I would be using them in books and took them on very low resolution. Some of my earlier photos are therefore of dubious quality and even more dubious creativity. There are only so many ways you can photograph a wall, especially with my old point and shoot colour camera. I reserve my real creativity for my black and whites.

Bits of the old Smiley Soldiers (that had always flanked the messages) were still visible for a while after, but the bridge was completely stripped and repainted in September 2006 in preparation for the re-introduction of train services, and the East London line now rolls across the bridge again every 5-10 minutes. I still romantically wonder if Banksy will be able to resist nostagicly targetting it again one day? Nostalgia isn't what it used to be you know.

This slogan was later used (on a sheet of metal) at the 'Barely Legal' exhibition in Los Angeles in September 2006. It presumably was sold there, as it later turned up at a weak exhibition of Banksy artworks in New York in December 2007.

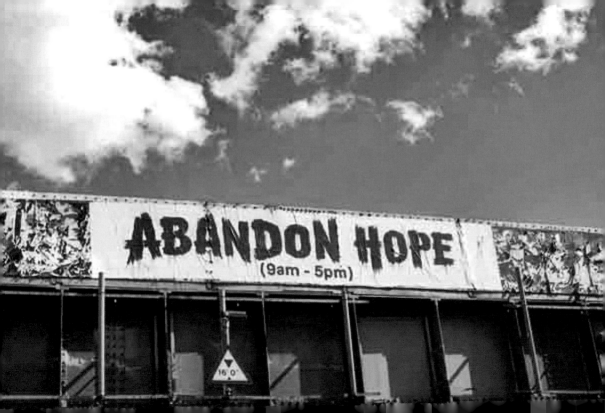

cutting rat

This was on the metal doors to one of the 'underneath the arches' workshops on Geffrye Street (Post Code - E2 8EA. Map/GPS reference - TQ 33573 83118), behind the lovely Geffrye Museum.

It was only one cutting rat this time, but because it was cutting into the padlock, it used the limiting context very effectively.

The half of the metal door with the Banksy on it was taken away in late February 2007. Wooden boards replaced it.

It later turned up in July 2009 at an awful 'exhibition' of ex-street works by Banksy in Covent Garden, London. It was shoddily entitled 'Please Love Me - Banksy' and contained a large amount of what they called 'architectural' pieces. I would call them ripped off street pieces.

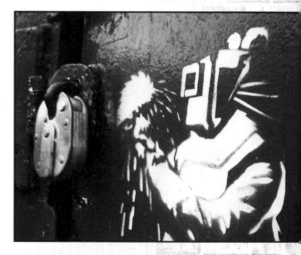

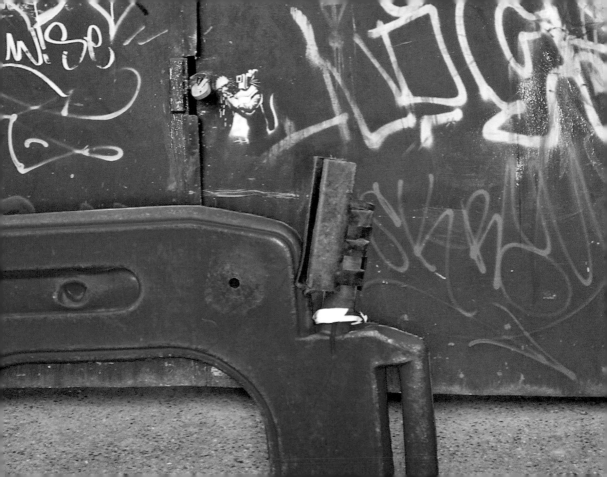

parachute rat

This was on a wall on the wonderfully entitled Diss Street (Post Code - **E2 7RA**. Map/GPS reference - **TQ 33712 82975**).

This was the best, and most photogenic parachute rat around until it fell foul of a Council clean up campaign in **December 2006**.

Several Eine'd shop shutters still exist on Hackney Rd, and the car park near Gorsuch Place is usually worth exploring for art.

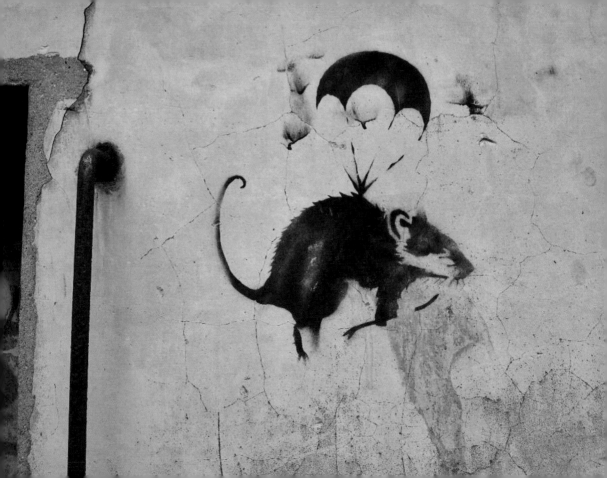

keep it real

This rare little monkey existed from at least mid 2005 towards the bottom of Ravenscroft Street, close to Columbia Road (Post Code - E2 7QB. Map/GPS reference - TQ 33927 82885)

There is only one rule in life. Yes, really... just one. You can never have enough monkeys.

That's it. Sorry if I have now spoiled the meaning of life for you, but you would find out sooner or later. Oh, and whilst I'm making peoples' lives better I'll let you into a secret. The tooth fairies don't really leave you money in return for your teeth; it's your parents.

Never the greatest piece of art (it was always rather small and hence the detail was poor) but for a long time it was the only surviving example around.

There is a photo of a similar monkey in 'Wall and Piece'. Whilst that may not be conclusive evidence that this one is 'real', it does bode well. We'll probably never definatively know.

It was buffed around December 2006.

BLT TIP

If you like tattoos, check out the Happy Sailor Tattoo shop at the bottom of Hackney Road (near Austin Street) which used to have several personalised Banksy prints on their walls.

Also check out the Shangri-La tattoo parlour at 54 Kingsland Road (by the rail bridge).

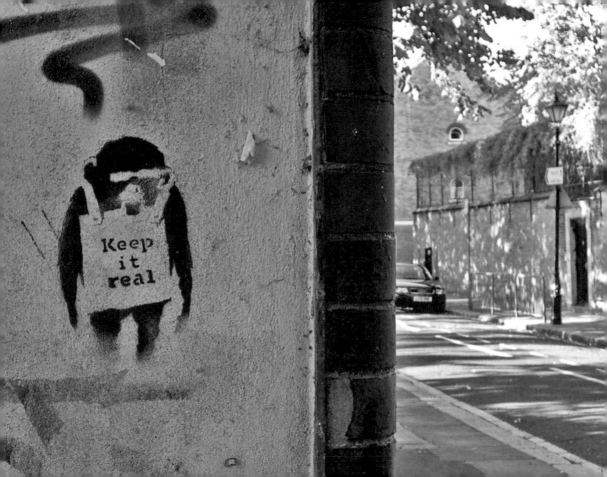

S25

the cargo area

Cargo - Post Code - EC2A 3AZ
Map/GPS reference - TQ 33374 82586

Location - Rivington Street near Shoreditch High Street (A10)

Cargo was often referred to as a super club but its night time reputation has dropped dramatically recently. It has pretty much supported Banksy from the start and two of his works still remain in the back courtyard, which shows great respect as most of the other walls in the courtyard are regularly rotated with new art.

Banksy has a huge amount of history with this site. After moving to the capital from Bristol he held his first London exhibition here in Spring 2001 just after Cargo opened. Large pieces occupied the walls of the open-air courtyard and the railway arch was white-washed, ready to use. 12 small pieces were sprayed on the south side along with the slogan 'Speak Softly. But Carry a Big Can of Paint'. 10 more pieces lived on the opposite wall. You could then order a canvas of any image from him.

Other parts of the walls were painted with repetitive images of (a) spiky haired cows, with earrings, and (b) billboard monkeys, declaring 'Lying to the police is never wrong' and 'Laugh now but one day we'll be in charge'. Slightly strangely, part of one of the spiky haired cows resurfaced in late 2009, and could momentarily be seen again, next to the main entrance. It's now covered again, by a Cargo advertising board.

As much of the exhibition began to fade away under the railway arch, Banksy re-visited and drew a huge couple with bright red lips. A large 'Thug For Life' bunny was sprayed in spring 2004. It was half buffed in September, but an amended version survived there until Spring 2005.

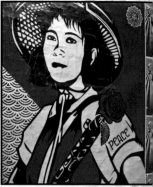

Shepard Fairey/Obey Giant paste-up the Cargo courtyard, circa 2006

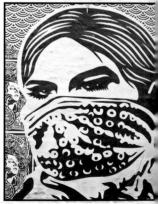

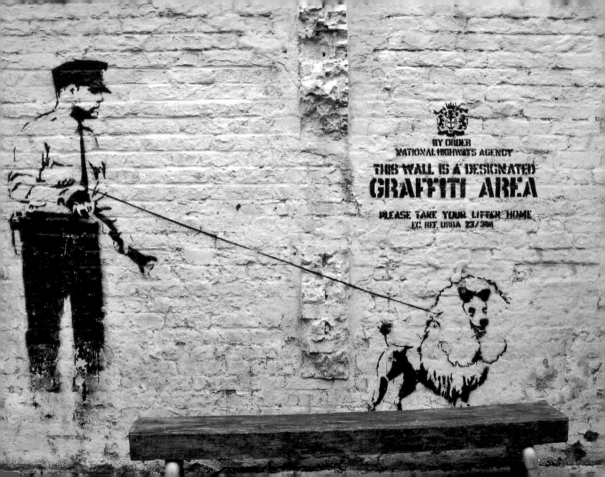

As if to mark his territory even more than an aggressive tomcat with incontinence, a huge Banksy tag was also added on the then disused train bridge above.

In the meantime Cargo continued to take good care of the art in the courtyard.

Two of the original 2001 walls still exist. The Guard and Poodle (and designated graffiti area) are on the first wall. A few walls away Banksy's HMV image remains, although for most of its life it has also been surrounded by graf from Stylo of the VOP crew - check out www.vopstars.com (Nipper, the dog the HMV logo was based on, was from Bristol, so maybe there's a connection there?)

The courtyard is open - for free - when the club isn't charging for entrance to the main club, although since they added wooden decking and loads of greenery in mid 2006 the walls have been harder to see and photograph. In March 2007 both of the courtyard Banksy's were covered with plastic, reminiscent of the sanitised 'street art' at the Old Truman Brewery. Wooden booth type seating has also been added in front of the HMV piece, which is rather detrimental to the piece.

Status - Still fine (October 2013)

A brief mention of two buffed pieces -

Just outside the club entrance, a slightly forlorn 'kid with paint brush' lurked under the arch for a short time in 2006 (see photo overleaf; now the site of Eine's gob smackingly fantastic 'Scary' piece) until badly buffed in November. Of the four times this image was used around London in May 2006 (see the BLT tip between F8 and F9 for one, and BLT Vol 2 for the other two), this one seemed to be the least finished, and in the least well chosen environment. I wonder if it was a job rushed or half finished?

Finally there was a 'Designated Picnic Area' and arrow in an alley (Standard Place) a stone's throw from Cargo (Map/GPS reference - TQ 33363 82594). It was there since at least September 2003 and originally pointed to a circle on the floor. The chrome and black dubs that surrounded it actually enhanced it in my opinion. A close-up view is shown over the page, and a context shot (complete with abandoned sofa) can be seen next to 'The Geeky Bit' page at the start of the book.

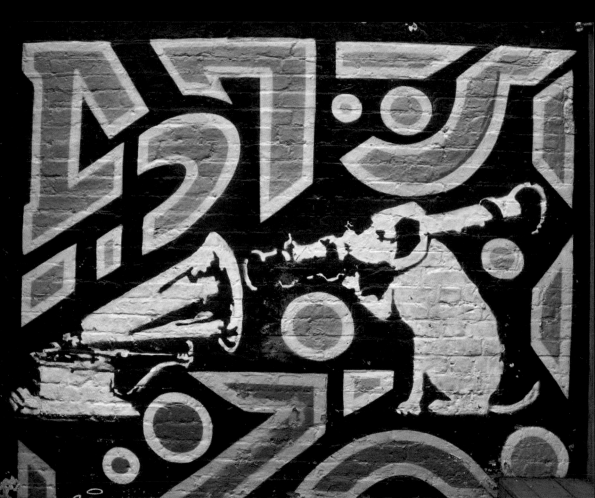

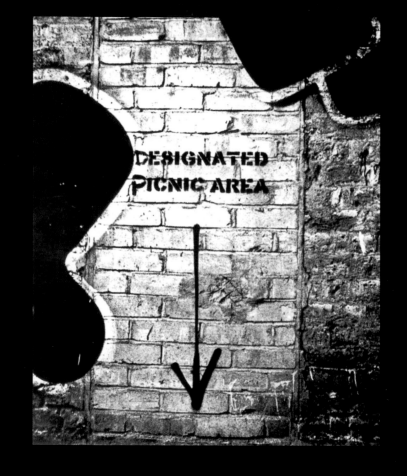

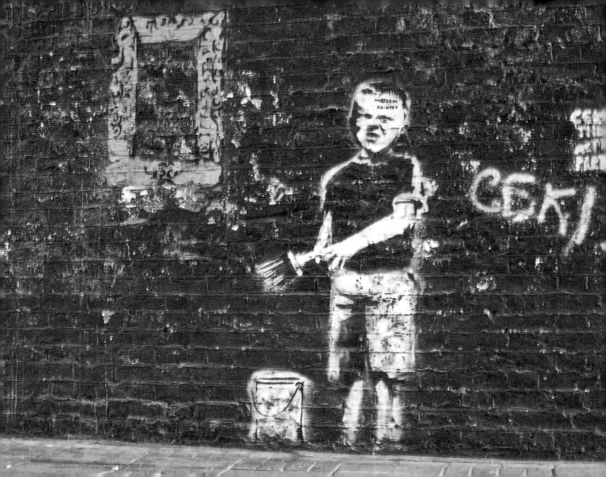

banksy tag

This used to be on the Turville Street side of 'Anisha Cash & Carry', on Redchurch Street (Post Code - E2 7HX. Map/GPS reference - TQ 33741 82409)

By the time I took my photos of it only the Banksy tag survived (inside the utilities box), but the reason the tag was there was because a lovely sawing rat used to exist just above the box. Have a look at Banksy's 'Existencilism' book to see what it looked like before. A photo of it was also briefly featured in his Oscar nominated film 'Exit Through the Gift Shop'.

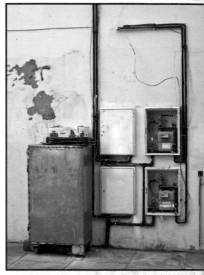

I thought it had been painted over in early-ish 2008, but later it transpired that the box had actually been removed, and that what I saw was a new box. How can I deduce this? Well, in January 2009, the box was offered for sale on 'Gumtree', the popular Aussie/Kiwi/Saffa/Hippie layabout web site. Also it had apparently been on eBay before; although I didn't see that. The cheeky monkey even referenced my book as some sort of provenance (see the early pages of the book for my rant about people who do that!). However, being in my book doesn't mean it is by Banksy. Only he can positively confirm or deny that; and quite rightly he will not. So there is no real provenance for street pieces. They belong on the streets.

The whole side wall was covered in some sweet graf by Probs and Kause in October 2009 (see bottom inset photo) and since then this wall has been regularly used for top drawer pieces.

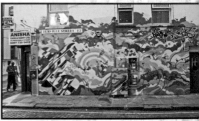

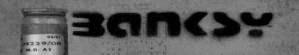

parachute rat

This rat was on the side of an old building on Sclater Street, on the junction with the Bethnal Green Road (A1209) (Post Code - E1 6HT. Map/GPS reference - TQ 33733 82291)

When Banksy originally did the rat there in 2003 the wall was fresh.

After I took this photo in 2006 it remained as a slowly fading rat for many years, sometimes hidden by the overgrowth. It was finally painted over sometime in 2009.

There used to be an ever changing gallery of street art along the semi-legal wall opposite this rat, often including large pieces by one of my favourite writers, CEPT (see inset photos for just two examples of his work). That wall is often bare now but the rest of the Sclater Street area is still very much painted, especially the car park.

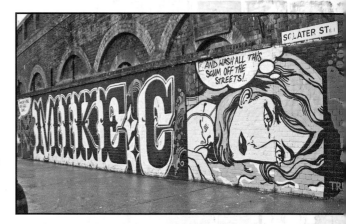

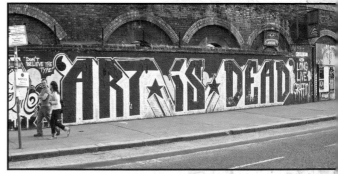

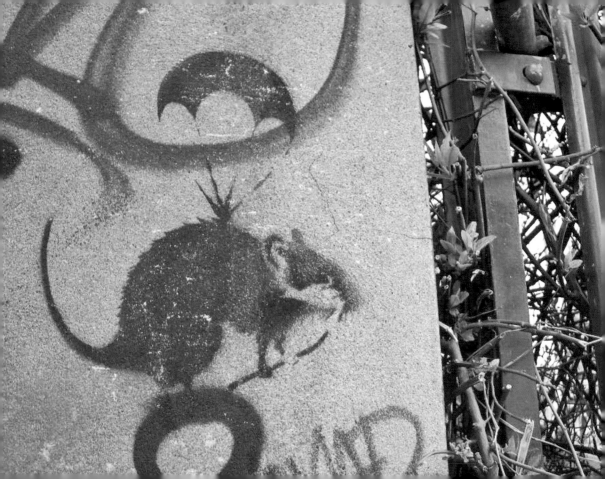

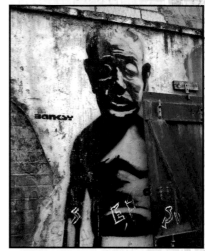

parachute rat

A good parachute rat existed here from at least early 2005 amidst the gallery of street art and eclectic market shops along Grimsby Street (Post Code - E2 6ES. Map/GPS reference - TQ 33930 82233).

Tentacles were added to it in Spring 2006 by a person unknown, but by the Autumn of the year it had almost all disappeared (see the bottom inset photo).

This whole side of the street was boarded up in 2007 so the East London train line could be extended, and the entire area was demolished in early 2008, never to be seen again.

Don't be fooled if you see old photos (like my top inset photo) of a small Banksy tag on the wall further down the street. The large alien/baby figures that used to exist nearby were **NOT** by Banksy. They were by Mr.Yu, a Japanese artist. The tag apparently related to a Banksy piece that used to be there. I didn't see the wall when it was there though and have never managed to find out exactly which of his pieces was there.

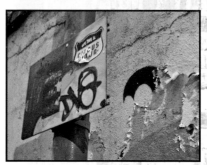

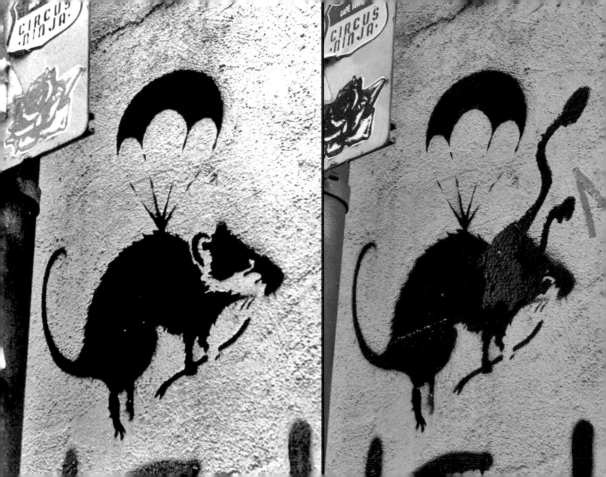

to advertise here call 0800 Banksy

This was towards the north end of Brick Lane, by the old (now closed) Shoreditch tube station (Post Code - E2 6ES. Map/GPS reference - TQ 33911 82220).

This exact piece is shown in Banksy's 'Wall and Piece' book, and had been there since at least late 2002. Seeing this in the flesh was a great sight whilst it lasted, with Eine's version opposite (see inset photo). When in this area be careful of the achingly laughable Shoreditch fashion victims and the Sunday street sellers ☺

It all went downhill when they started the extension to the East London train line. In March 2007 a temporary bridge was placed right over both the hoardings (i.e. both Banksy & Eine) and the two wooden sections that contained the 'ban' and 'ksy' words quickly went missing. Most of the rest of the Banksy slogan followed soon afterwards.

Part of these hoardings (just the 'Banksy' bit) later turned up in July 2009 at an awful 'exhibition' of ex-street works by Banksy in Covent Garden, London. It was woefully entitled 'Please Love Me - Banksy' and contained a large amount of what they called 'architectural' pieces (others would call them ripped off street pieces).

BLT TIP

Sadly this area has really been tidied up since the book first came out, but the walls down to the old tube station are usually still worth checking out.

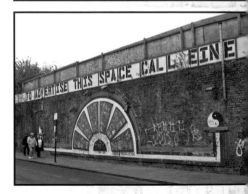

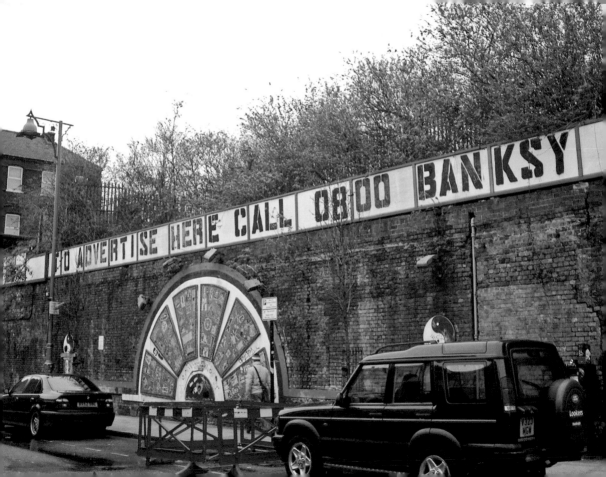

CCTV pole

This was on Brick Lane, opposite the side entrance to the old Truman Brewery (Post Code - E1 5HD / Map/GPS reference - TQ 33893 82003).

Banksy hit several **CCTV** poles around London, putting up plastic rooks holding pirate flags and cigarettes, and pulling at fake electrical wiring. How do I know they are rooks? Well, as we say in the sticks, 'If ye sees a rook, that be a crow. If ye sees lots of crows, thems be rooks'.

A Banksy tag existed on this pole, so I imagine that this was one of those sites at some point in the past. A very similar situation still exists at a **CCTV** pole on Tottenham Court Road, where a Banksy tag still exists but nothing else. See BLT Vol.2 for full details.

For many years the tag survived without any rooks on the pole (which funnily enough was smeared all over with 'anti-climb paint'), but even the tag was eventually painted over sometime between November 2010 and May 2011.

A small canvas of birds pulling at wires on a **CCTV** pole was on sale at Santa's Ghetto (Pictures on Walls' Christmas shop) in 2003.

In July 2003 a similar image was created by Banksy for the cover artwork of a 'Badmeaningood' compilation - Vol 4, by the Scratch Perverts on the Ultimate Dilemma label - Cat No. **UDR CD 021 (CD)** and **UDR LP 021 (Vinyl)**. It is pretty hard to find these days.

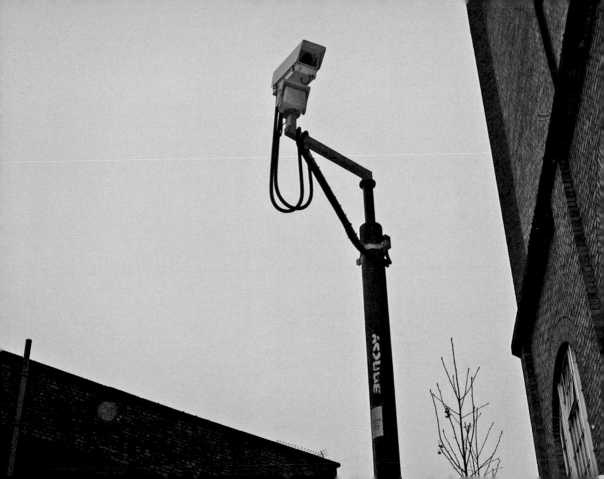

gas mask girl

This girl was on Brick Lane, at the corner with Woodseer Street since at least 2003 (Post Code - E1 5HD / Map /GPS reference - **TQ 33895 81983**).

She slowly faded away over the years, and was often attacked by the remnants of fly posters, until a final demise in 2013.

Note the very faint 'Banksy' tag by the girls right foot. Rather strangely the tag was resprayed, circa early 2012, but it was done with a smaller stencil. Some people postulated that one of the annoying 'street art tours' in the area may have done it to make it look more attractive to punters.

A rather surreal 'woman' playing a violin (with a happy chopper in a thought bubble - as you do - I always dream about war when playing the violin...) used to be just a few metres away along this wall.

About 100 metres away, on the massive wall opposite the Hanbury Street entrance to the Old Truman Brewery, a faded Grin Reaper used to exist. By the time I took the photo on the right in early 2006 it was already almost dead. It faded away totally over the next year.

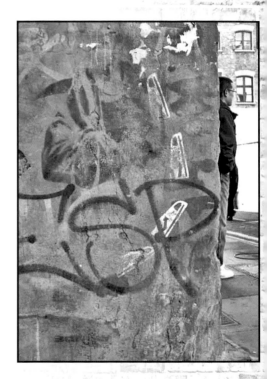

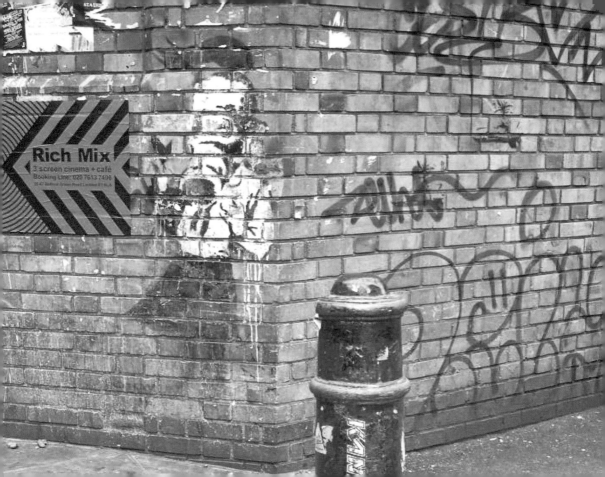

pink car & death driver

Post Code - E1 5HD   Map/GPS reference - TQ 33893 82003

Location & some History - On top of an old shipping container, in the main concourse area of the old Truman Brewery yard. A photo of it is shown in the 'Wall and Piece' book.

I've never quite found out the reason for it, but an old Triumph Spitfire GT6 was given a Banksy treatment. The car has existed there since at least April 2004, when it was originally an Orange colour, but it wasn't until some time in late 2004/early 2005 that Mr.B did his paint job on it. A good photographic history of the site exists on the Banksy group on flickr.

A Banksy tag still exists on the far right of the container, although like the car it is also now covered by a sheet of transparent plastic.

Many photographers make sure they get the 'Gherkin' (Swiss Re buillding) in the background if they take a photo of this. I'm more of a realist so I prefered to get the skanky derelict alchy/graffiti/drugs den in the background. It's on Grey Eagle Street, but has long been locked up.

In Feb/March 2008 the window from the car disappeared and a piece of wood then covered up the hole. Apparently it was smashed, rather than stolen. But it had also been seen several years previously without the window, so I'm not sure if on the first occasion it had permanently gone, meaning that the most recent one was actually the 2nd version anyway? I'm confused. I can see biscuits. Fly my little munchkin, fly! Nurse, give me another brace of those lovely red pills please.

Pieces by Space Invader, Dscreet, and Shepard Fairey/Obey Giant, plus D*face's rival car (see inset photo), can usually also be seen in the old Truman Brewery yard, or just outside it.

Status - The car is still there (October 2013), but since late 2006 it has been covered with a nasty see through box, and as the dirt has gathered on it over many years it's become a real eyesore.

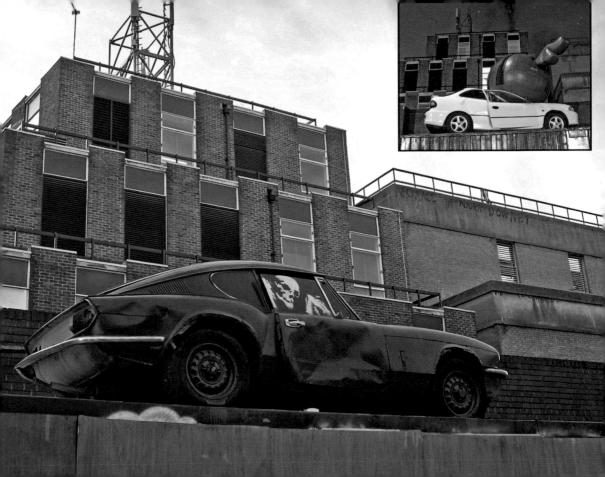

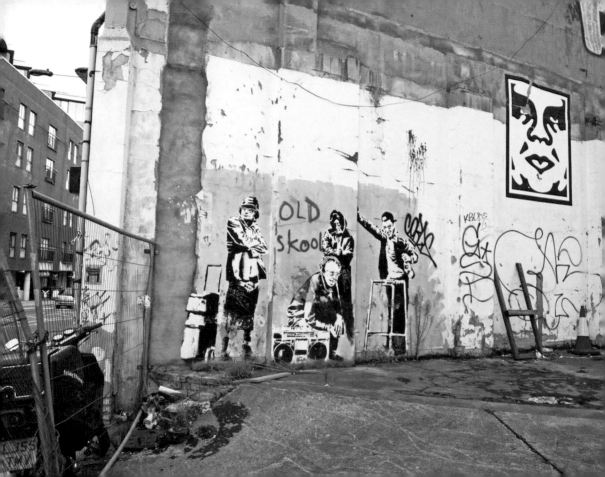

Farringdon & Clerkenwell

I did this free mini-tour for the public in mid 2006, and at the time it included oodles of excellent quality rats (especially in the Barbican area that I called 'rat city'), as well as the Cash Machine & Girl, Thugs for Life (or 'old skool' as some know it) and two enormous Blek Le Rat indoor pieces.

Over the years most have gone, although several do remain and are well worth the visit if you can.

The tour took less than two hours. It went around the Barbican/Smithfields area first, before heading up to Clerkenwell and Hatton Garden, and continuing via the Farringdon Road and Exmouth Market to end by the enormous Mount Pleasant postal sorting office.

After BLT was published a new Banksy arrived relatively close to the start of the original tour, so for the 4th edition I added the 'ratapult' into the book, as location F1.

But just as I finished the book, I revisited it and found that it had already gone! Classic.

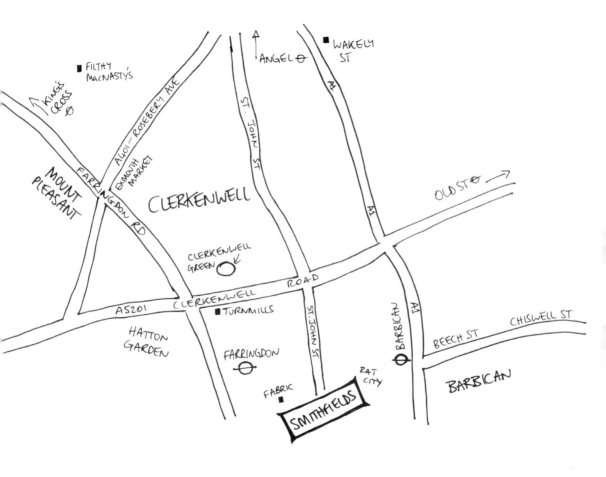

ratapult

This was on the wall outside the 'East House' Chinese takeaway on Whitecross Street (near the junction with Roscoe Street - Map/GPS reference - **TQ 32382 82250**).

A man at a local business confirmed to me that this was not there in the late evening of Saturday 8th September 2007, but was mysteriously there by early next morning. It was one of three new pieces that went up in London that weekend. The others were the 'Old St Cherub' - location S12 - and the Portobello Market version of 'Nob Artiste' - see **BLT Vol 2**

Over the following days, weeks and years, several additions were made to the wall, including the red 'target' lines and the wavy black line in my photo of it, which was taken just a few days after it was done, but none seriously detracted from the piece until one larger one on the right hand side in April 2009. In mid April the serial graffiti 'vandal' 10foot continued his dogging spree of Banksy pieces with a throw up between the rat and the cat, and after that it got regularly hit, added to and then cleaned up.

Between March and June 2010 the wall was totally whitewashed, and a dainty little wall garden was built in front of it. Goodbye rat, hello shrubbery.

The photo of it on Banksy's web site called it 'ratapult' & was accompanied with the following text, **"RAT FACT - In London you're never more than 20 feet away from somebody telling you you're never more than 20 feet away from a rat"**.

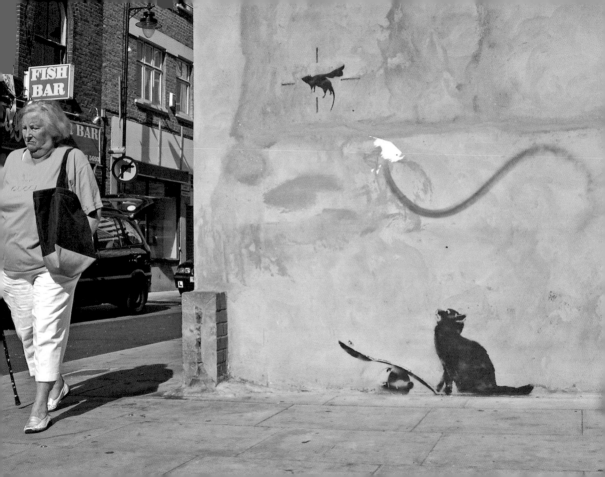

placard rat - 'london doesn't work'

Post Code - EC1Y 4SB   Map / GPS reference - TQ 32497 81970

Location -   Chiswell Street, near Lamb's Passage.

This is an exceptional example of Banksy's placard rat image, this time announcing that 'London Doesn't Work'. A photo of it was briefly featured in his Oscar nominated film 'Exit Through the Gift Shop'.

This rat has been there since at least January 2004 and was one of the most popular black & white photos that I sold. In a stroke of genius I took my original photo of it with a London taxi going past; surely one of the iconic images of London, not that I'm saying taxi drivers are what makes London 'not work'. Johnny 'The Knuckles' Wilson wouldn't let me say that and nor would my dear departed Dad, who was a taxi driver for much of his life.

Unfortunately it was a silver taxi and not the black version! Tough. Take your own photo if you prefer, clever clogs.

In late February 2010 the placard was amended to read, in chunky black marker pen, 'I Love Robbo', presumably as part of the fallout from the now infamous 'Robbo' incident, when Banksy amended/went over a very old piece by veteran writer Robbo on the Regent's Canal in Camden. Shortly afterwards it was amended again to 'I ♥ London Robbo'.

Status - Apart from the (Team) 'Robbo' addition, it has had a surprisingly small amount of dogging around it, and still looks great (October 2013). The only problem is that a small metal parking post has been conspicuously fixed to the left of the rat.

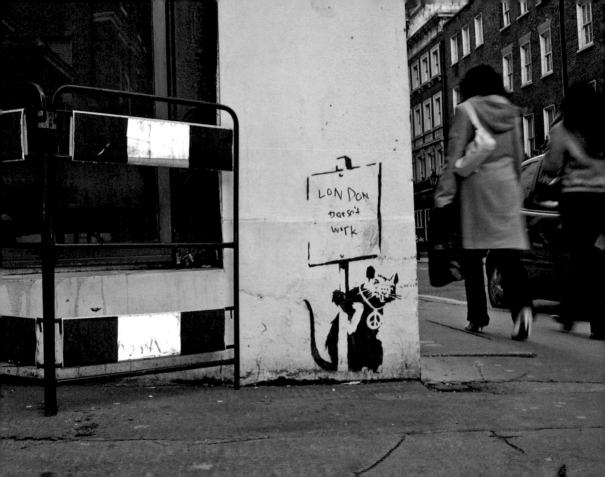

faded placard rat

Post Code - EC1A 9HF
Map / GPS reference - TQ 32065 81844

Location & Whatever Else I Can Think of (without trying too hard of course...)

On Long Lane, just around the corner from Barbican tube station.

A very faded placard rat. Hardly worth mentioning, but it is a good example of how this one (on the main road) was swiftly buffed to within an inch of its life, whereas the gaggle of rats (or litter, or gang, or parliament, or whatever the term of venery it is) around the corner (see F4) were treated as preserved works of art for several years.

Status

Hard to see, even if you know where it is (October 2013)

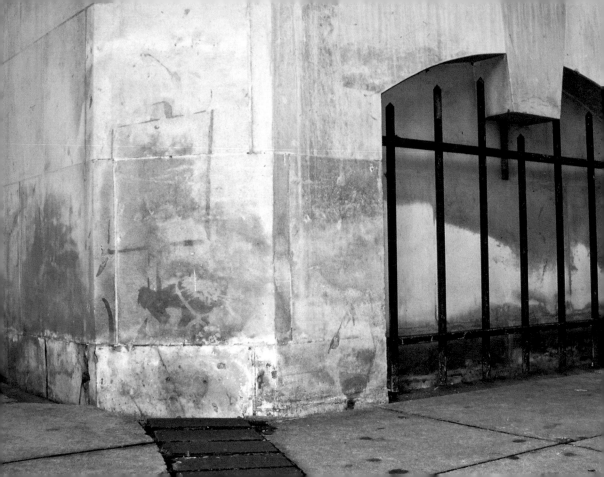

the rat pack

These four rats all used to be within 20 metres of each other, around Hayne Street and Charterhouse Square (Post Code - EC1A 9HG. Map/GPS reference - TQ 31941 81847).

Banksy obviously had a bit of a mentalist moment in the Barbican area one night. By daybreak four stencils adorned the local walls within a stones throw of each other.

The 'Go Back to Bed' placard rat was on Hayne Street & it spoke very personally to me when it told us to go back to bed. Very sound advice. I'm more of a no-getter than a go-getter.

The other three (see photos) were all on the same building on Charterhouse Square and when it got repainted (twice; first pink, see inset photo of the Gangsta Rat, and then white) they actually painted around the Banksy pieces, thus preserving them a little while longer.

The second placard rat originally (circa early 2004) was painted without a slogan. Later 'welcome to hell' then appeared on it. The body of the rat later had 'Go back to Bristol boy' scrawled onto it by a person unknown (see final photo). The red '4' stencil on top seems to have been a viral advertising campaign for 'Resident Evil 4'.

Three of them (all except the 'Bling Rat') are shown in Banksy's books.

Two of them ('Go Back To Bed', and the 'Bling Rat') were painted over in December 2007. Then in January 2008 I received an anonymous email telling me the other two ('Gangsta Rat' and 'Welcome to Hell') had been "surgically removed from the wall and replaced with fresh plaster". These rats were dying like flies (if that isn't a mixed metaphor).

It wasn't until November 2009 that a slightly crazy story emerged (in Vice Magazine) about the incompetant theft, and resultant destruction, of the gangsta rat. If the story is true the phrase 'surgically removed' suddenly becomes rather funny/painful as it ended in the death of this likeable piece. This one was my favourite gangsta rat in London, and was the same stencil that was used for the official screenprint from Pictures On Walls (POW).

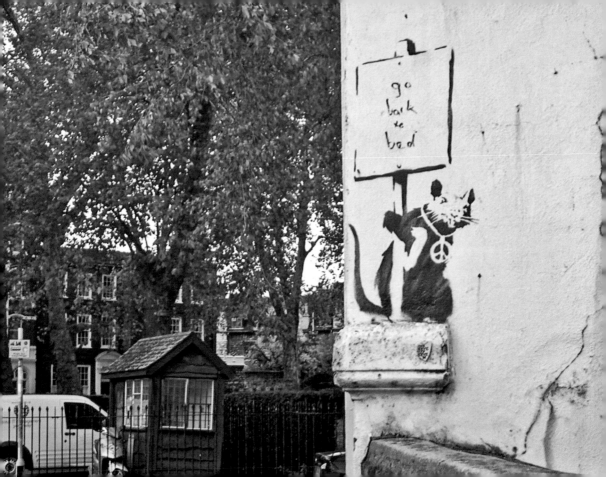

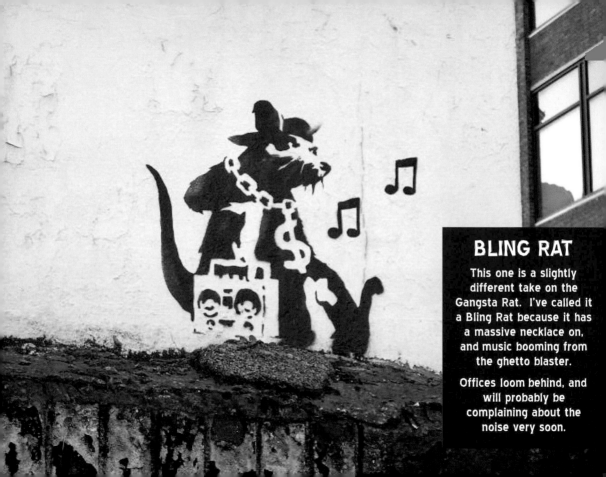

BLING RAT

This one is a slightly different take on the Gangsta Rat. I've called it a Bling Rat because it has a massive necklace on, and music booming from the ghetto blaster.

Offices loom behind, and will probably be complaining about the noise very soon.

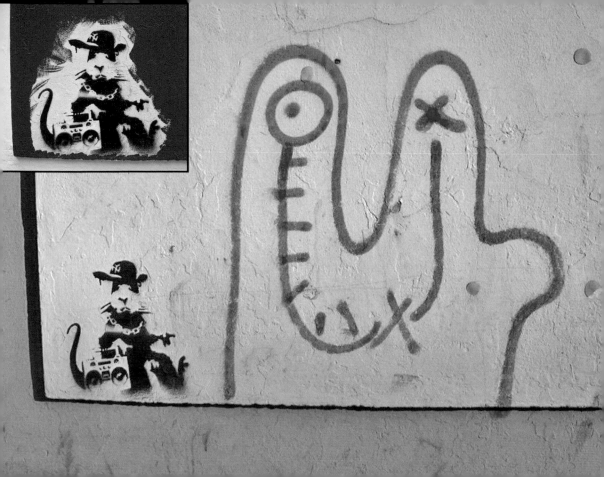

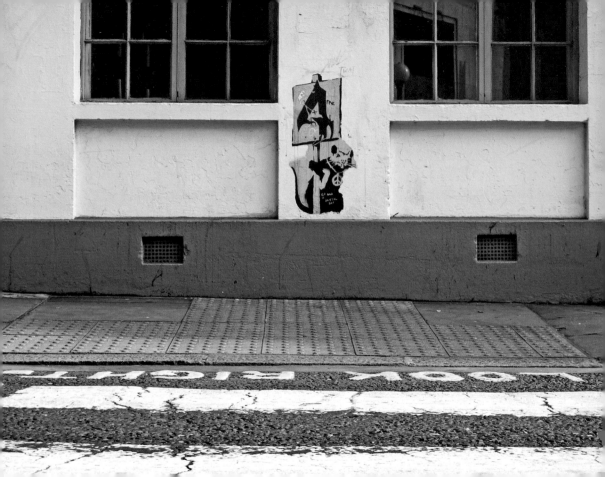

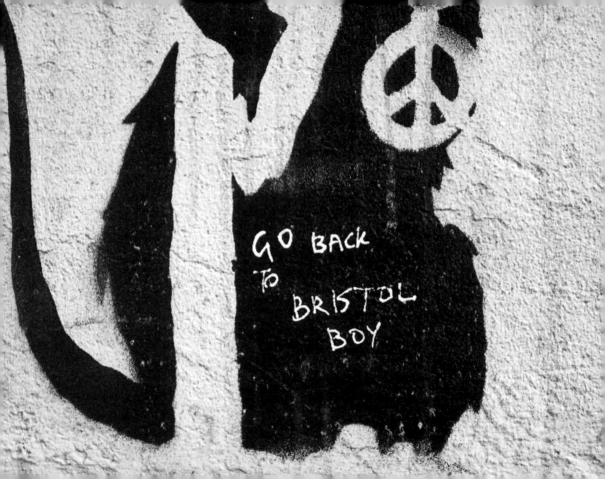

faile + stencils

Two fantastically detailed stencils ('Smoking' and 'Monster') from the Faile crew were executed in Lindsey Street, on the wall of an old 'Men's Lavatory' opposite the East side of Smithfields Market (Post Code - EC1A 9HL. Map/GPS reference - TQ 31943 81802).

I spotted these early in June 2006, but they might have actually been part of the Faile blitz in late May 2006 when the Faile collective plastered Shoreditch with various examples of their name, and snarling dog wheatpastes.

At this time Faile may still have just been in their original incarnation as a collective of three people; a Canadian man, an American man and a Japanese woman, operating out of New York. Around this time Aiko left, but the two Patrick's (i.e. the men) continued on. For more info see www.faile.net

A ham-fisted attempt was made to buff it in early 2007 (see inset photo).

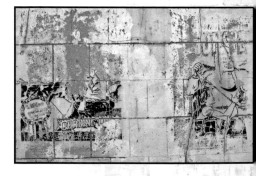

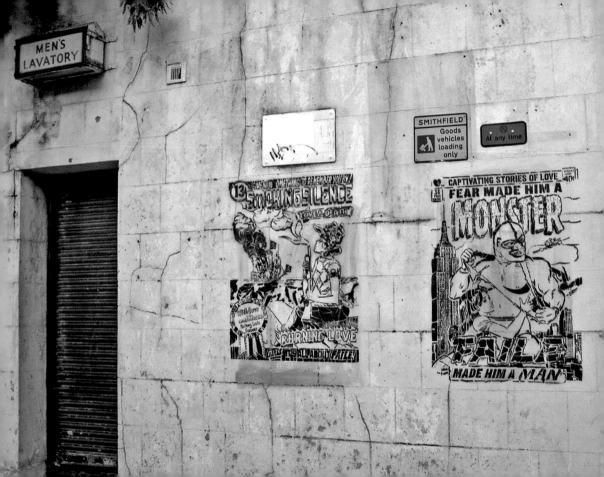

bomb hugger

Map/GPS reference - TQ 31709 81783

Location & Possibly Helpful Padding

Inside 'Fabric' club, 77a Charterhouse Street, EC1M 3HN.

For all you drum n bass heads out there, a night out at Fabric will not only make your jinglies jangle, but you can also check out an original Banksy Bomb Hugger that he sprayed straight onto the wall, by the toilets.

The club even put a real frame around it.

Status

Still there I presume? I'm too miserable for Fabric now I reckon.

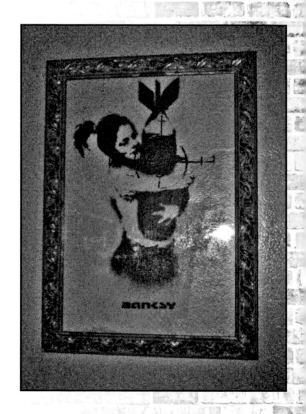

HISTORIC BLT TIP

On your way up St. John's Street (between locations F7 and F8) you used to be able to check out a road sign that had large Obey Giant and D*face paste-ups on it (see inset photo - left). The whole sign was removed in early 2007 during the infamous Pol Pot inspired 'Signpost Year Zero' pogroms.

You can still just about glimpse a large Blek Le Rat paste up (see inset photo - right) inside an old empty shop on the east side of St. John's Street, approx opposite Aylesbury Street. An even more enormous piece, a 'Drummer Girl' canvas (official title = 'Resist Against the Imposters'), lived in the clothes shop next door but in late 2007 the whole shop closed down, and the Blek canvas had gone.

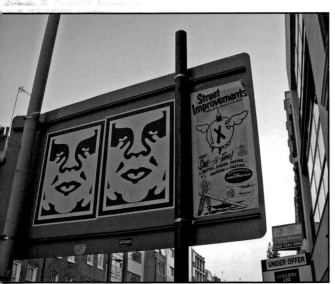

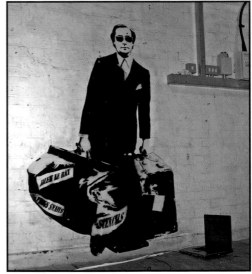

gangsta rat

This was at floor level, near some railings on Peter's Lane (just off St. John's Street) (Post Code - EC1M 4BL. Map / GPS reference - TQ 31772 81903)

Yeah yet another rat, but another good quality one and it had a very perculiar addition to it. Someone had written 'not a banksy' on it, when in fact it looked like one of the clearest Banksy's around. Sure, they can be faked (and there were some questionable ones out there), but I doubt this one was. And it had been there since at least 2004, which at least firmly put it in a realistic timeframe for possible authenticity as rat stencils haven't generally been done by Banksy for many years now, and all new-ish ones are therefore usually fake.

Repetitious images of a woman's face were added to the right of it in early 2007, and later in the year various other daubs were added, including a supporting comment that it was 'a proper Banksy'.

The wall was completely whitewashed in mid March 2008. There are photos on the Banksy group on flickr showing workmen whilst they did it. Now you are more likely to find a pool of Friday night sick where it used to be.

The buildings on the opposite side of St. John's Street were used as the 'Trans-Siberian Restaurant' in David Cronenberg's excellent 2007 film 'Eastern Promises'. One of Eine's shop shutters in Broadway Market (Hackney) also featured in the opening scenes of the movie.

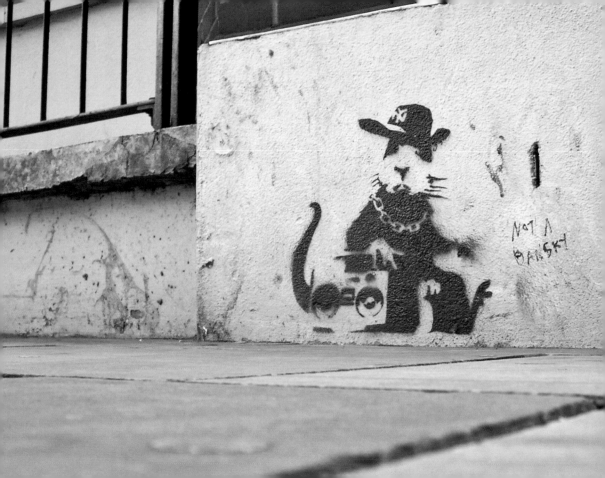

refuse store hanging rat

Previously at the bottom end of Agdon Street (just off St. John's Street / Compton Street - Post Code - EC1V 4JY. Map/GPS reference - **TQ 31688 82363**).

I loved the placement of this likkle rat, hanging off a door marked 'Refuse Store'. The metal door gave photo's of it a grey tone, but if you play around with the image you can also get it into a nice contrasty black and white image.

The rat looks exactly the same as several images of these rats in Banksy's various books.

When I walked past in the pouring rain in early January 2008 (the things I do to update this book!) I noticed the whole door had gone, and a wooden door had been set up behind the original metal door (see inset photo below). Photos I later saw on the Internet suggested it might have already been gone in November 2007.

I speculated in the 3rd edition of this book that it might soon be seen for sale on eBay. I wasn't far wrong as it turned up at the Contemporary Art auction on 27th September 2008 by the previously well respected Scottish auctioneer 'Lyon & Turnball'.

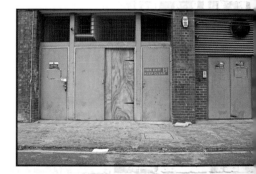

This was one of their first ever auctions in London, and was the first to contain lots of street art. It controversially contained five Banksy street pieces, all allegedly authenticated by 'Vermin', a company that 'authenticates' Banksy street works even though they have no input from Banksy, Pictures on Walls or Pest Control (the company given permission by Banksy to authenticate his work).

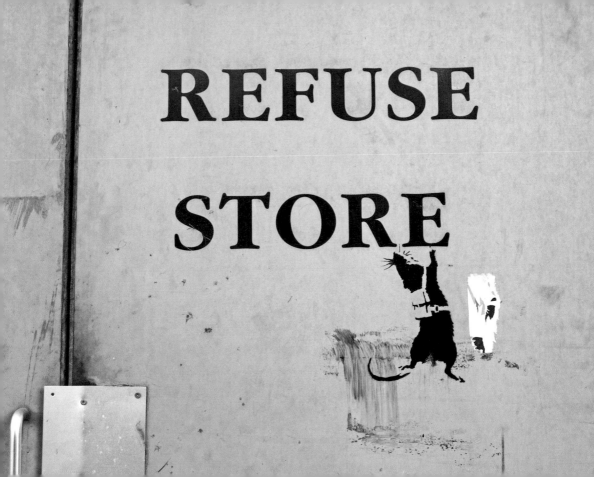

I was very very unhappy when a friend told me that they had referenced this book in their sales description of the piece. I rattled off a complaint to Lyon & Turnball, but they refused to take out their reference to BLT. My follow up emails went unanswered, which wasn't wholly unexpected, especially as the third one was childishly smug that their auction had been a colossal flop.

My argument went like this (almost verbatim). 1) you use my book as some sort of claim to give provenance to your piece. My book is not meant for this. It is meant as a reference book and DIY guide. It is not a sales catalogue, nor a map to find what pieces to steal, take to auction or buy from the owner; 2) you are selling a street piece and trying to make a huge amount of money from it; 3) you are using 'Vermin' as some sort of provenance for your piece, when they actually know little. Banksy and Pest Control are the only people that can provide provenance, and they will not give provenance on street pieces because they don't want to. Is that an accident? No, it's because street pieces are meant for the street. Are you getting the message yet? Most people do not want to see street pieces being sold by auction houses.

Compare and contrast the following news stories to see how they started off so bullish (especially about the use of 'Vermin') and ended up with 80% of the lots failing to sell.

- http://news.bbc.co.uk/1/hi/scotland/edinburgh_and_east/7596740.stm
- http://news.bbc.co.uk/1/hi/entertainment/7638493.stm
- http://news.bbc.co.uk/1/hi/entertainment/7641966.stm

The estimate price of the door was £20-25,000, but it went unsold. I felt vindicated to a degree.

This story still had a few twists up its sleeve though. After failing to sell it then turned up at the appropriately named Bankrobber Gallery. At least that finally gave us some clarity about Vermin, as their web site (which was shared with Bankrobber at this point) conclusively began to state, "From 2009 Vermin recognizes Bankrobber as the only commercial outlet for Vermin certified works", and several street pieces were being openly offered for sale by Bankrobber.

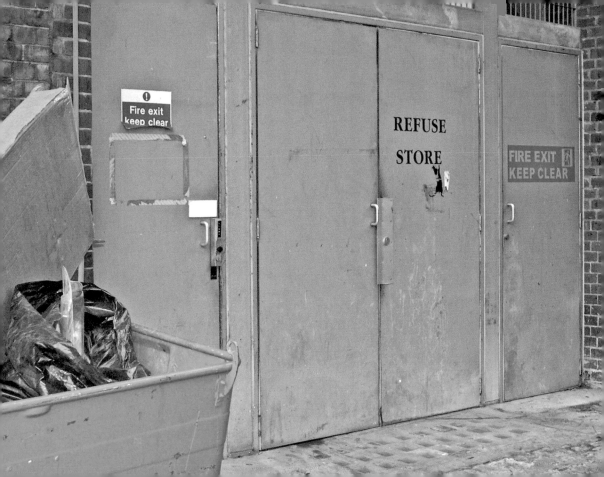

BLT TIP - Banksy vs. faile

This was originally only in BLT as a detour, because it was a fair old poke off the normal tour route. It was on Wakely Street (A501), by the corner with Goswell Road (Postcode - EC1V 7RQ), and was not only another great example of Banksy's 'kid' stencil, which he used at least four times in London in May 2006, but also a great faile stencil ('Fate'), and a timeless vision of 'dangerous' urban decay in an otherwise gentrified area.

In January 2008 both were boarded up and the Banksy was offered for sale on eBay. The faile would graciously be thrown in for free; like a silent fart in a small room. The seller said the building was being developed, and that he had permission to sell it. They also wrote that, "This is a once in a lifetime chance to rescue and own a part of the real London", which is surely irony if I ever heard it. Bidding finished at Ł8,100, whichdidn't meet the seller's reserve.

Both remained heavily boarded up for a long time, but the Banksy must have been physically taken off the building, as it turned up in July 2009 at an awful 'exhibition' of ex-street works by Banksy in Covent Garden, London. It was shoddily entitled 'Please Love Me - Banksy' and contained a large amount of what they called 'architectural' pieces. I would call them ripped off street pieces. It was later being touted by Bankrobber Gallery (see F8 above for a similar story). I hate giving them publicity, but I do have to document what happens to this piece.

Please remember kiddies that this book is **NOT** provenance that a piece featured here is by Banksy and can probably be sold for the price of a small house. This book is no guarantee that something is by Banksy, and it's supposed to help fans of his work find them, rather than help stymied buy-to-let landlords make an even quicker buck on the latest avaricious bubble.

If you are in the area and are thirsty you might like to stop off at Filthy MacNasty's at 68 Amwell Street, EC1. This pub is covered with music memorabilia, including some of favourite son Pete Doherty whilst he was with The Libertines, and plays an eclectic mix of music. Lenin reputedly drank here in 1905. He's probably not been back for a while though.

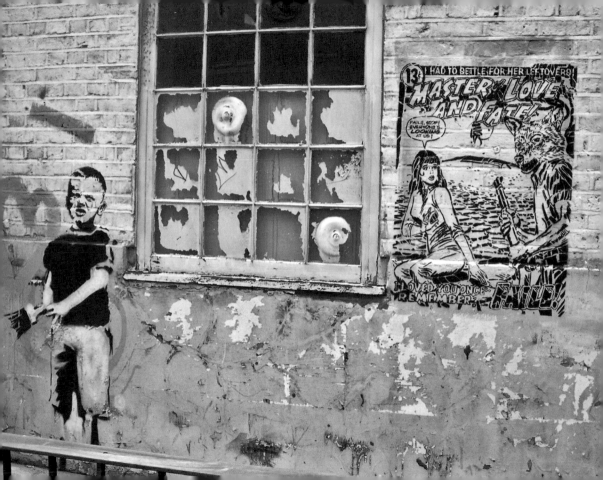

papa 'rat' zi

Parts of this can still be seen at the south end of Clerkenwell Close (i.e. close to Clerkenwell Green - Post Code - EC1R 0DY - Map/GPS reference - TQ 31494 82185) but because it is in such miserable condition I have considered it more of a 'dead' location. Visit if you really wish.

It is peculiarly tucked away on the side of some flats where few might be expecting to see this photographer-cum-rat.

One time when I was checking its status and taking a few new photos of it, I met the woman whose flat is beside it. She was amiable enough, but said she was sometimes disturbed by the attention it got, at all hours of the day and night. I didn't have the heart to tell her that I had written a book telling people how to find it.

Note that the 'Banksy' tag on the satchel is on backwards. Maybe a little drop of alcohol can seemingly make for a fun evening?

A reader of BLT kindly told me in October 2008 that it was still there, but that it now had about six blobs of bright coloured paint surrounding it. Strange. It looked like a tube of smarties had exploded over it.

JUSTICE

Banksy's 'Justice' statue was famously unveiled to a scrum of people on Clerkenwell Green in August 2004.

Nothing survives today though.

The statue was a modified version of the statue of Justice from the Old Bailey, including a blindfold and a garter with an American dollar bill tucked in it. A posh plaque on it read 'Trust No One'.

A statement was read out by MC Dynamite on Banksy's behalf: "It's the most honest depiction of British justice currently on display in the capital". Banksy apparently said 'I hope it stays there for good'.

The statue was taken away by the Council 2 days later.

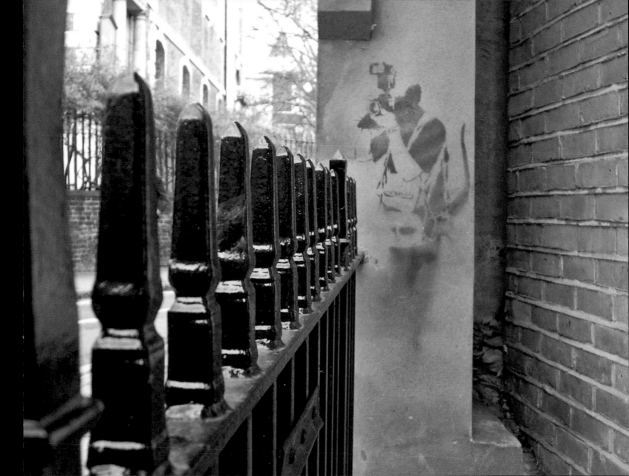

thugs for life (a.k.a. old skool)

This existed in a small car park on Clerkenwell Road (A5201), near Saffron Hill (Post Code - EC1R 5DL. Map/GPS reference - TQ 31299 82030). Before the pensioner thugs turned up in 2004 with their B-Boy gear and zimmer frames, a small rat writing 'Because I'm Worthless' existed on this wall. This large piece had various titles added above it over the years, including 'Thugs For Life' and 'Old Skool'. The massive, and painstaking, stencils to make up the piece are shown at the end of the hardback edition of 'Wall and Piece'.

In mid January 2008 an awful looking mish mash of metal hoardings suddenly covered the wall up. It reminded me of the shanty towns in Addis Ababa (Ethiopia) where I used to live. On the 26th February it was opened up again. The wall was now mainly blank, but had a Banksy-style 'cut out & collect' line around where the graffiti used to be, and had the word 'collected' stenciled in the middle, in large letters. Now that is what I call a beautifully sick sense of humour! Within a day this tongue-in-cheek message was whitewashed though.

On 4th March 2008, The Evening Standard ran a story about the removal, with a typically restrained headline; "Banksy, taken off wall by German, now worth Ł300,000", as if the buyers nationality was important.

The article wrote that, "Today, it emerged that... the owner of the garage has sold it - for Ł1,000. The buyer spent about Ł30,000 having the image 'peeled' from the wall by a specialist firm... The mural's new owner has chosen, like the artist, to remain anonymous but he is thought to be a German man in his 30's who works in advertising". Um, so not that anonymous then? ☺

It continued, "Olly Pugh, manager of Clerkenwell Motorcycles in Clerkenwell Road, insisted the building's owner was happy with the price he had agreed for the painting. He said: "No one knew too much about Banksy at the time and he thought, 'If some idiot is going to give me Ł1,000 for a mural that's great'. Part of the deal was that he will get a life-size reproduction of the mural." The picture was removed by Tom Organ of the Wall Paintings Workshop in Kent. It took Mr Organ, who normally helps restore medieval wall paintings, six weeks to complete. He said: "We stuck some film over the top of the mural with an adhesive and gradually cut and peeled away quarter-millimetre-thick sections of the paintwork. We put the pieces back together like a jigsaw on a new support and then removed the film with a solvent that wouldn't damage the paint. I think my client was looking for about six months before he found a conservation company that could do the job but the techniques have been around for years... It's ironic because I've spent most of my life trying to keep paintings on walls" ".

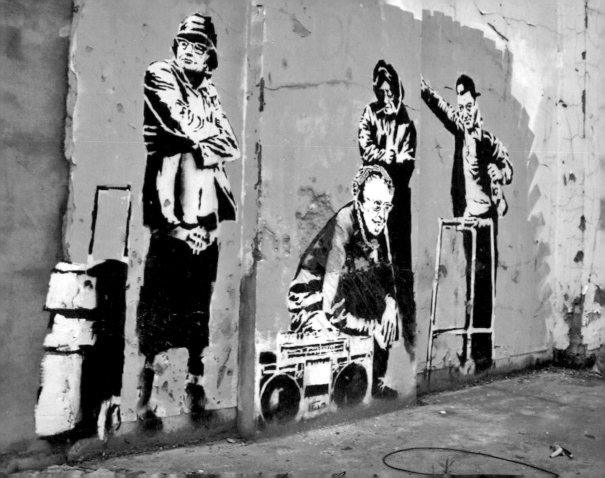

gangsta rat

This used to be on Roseberry Avenue (A401), very near the junction with Farringdon Road (A201) (Post Code - EC1R 4QD. Map/GPS reference - TQ 31193 82422).

It was on the metal delivery box of City News (4 Exmouth Market) from at least mid 2004, but in October 2006 it was reported that the whole box had been sold off by the shop. A nice shiny new one replaced it.

By November it was already being sold on eBay.

It was later shown at a certain West London gallery in Feb/March 2008. And also turned up in July 2009 at the infamously dire 'exhibition' of ex-street works in Covent Garden, London. It was shoddily entitled 'Please Love Me - Banksy' and contained a large amount of what they called 'architectural' pieces. Others would call them ripped off street pieces. If these public presentations continue I think I might have to rename it 'prostituted rat'.

Street pieces are meant for the streets, and were not made as conversation pieces in posh peoples' reception rooms.

A rather strange metal cube used to existed nearby in spring 2004. For no obvious reason it just sat there, by a tree next to the main road. It had a small Banksy umbrella rat added to it (like the one at location S8), but the whole thing soon disappeared. I wonder if someone out there has simultaneously the coolest, yet most uncomfortable, foot rest on the planet in their living room?

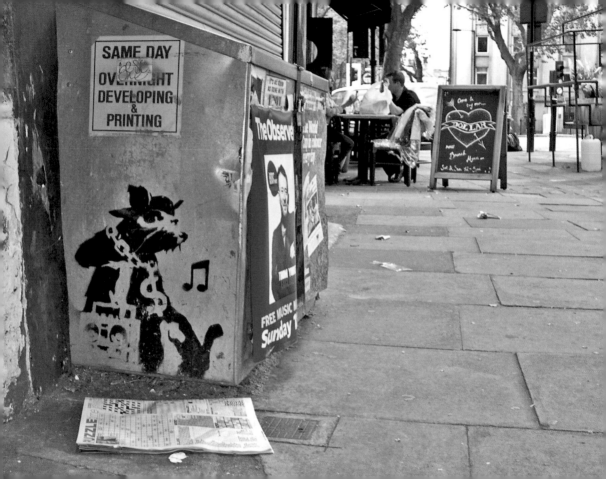

cash machine & girl

Post Code - WC1X 0DW
Map / GPS reference - TQ 31148 82454

Location & Seemingly Endless History & Chatter

Roseberry Avenue (A401), very near the junction with Farringdon Road (A201).

It's a cash machine with a mechanical arm grabbing a girl. What on earth does this mean?

Enough thinking time peeps... a long time ago this site started as just a small Banksy umbrella rat on an old disused window. The first photo I've seen of it was from April 2004, although it may have been there a bit earlier. By May 2004 a big black rain cloud had been added above it. I'm not sure if that was by Banksy or not, but it suited it well.

By Mid 2005 the window had been bricked up and the cash machine had been put up over it, with Banksy/D*face's 'di-faced tenners' (fake £10 notes with Princess Di on them instead of the Queen) spewing out of it. It was this 2005 incarnation that is shown in the 'Wall and Piece' best seller. The tenners didn't last long, and later in 2005 the arm and girl were added (see photo opposite).

Wasn't that history lesson interesting? I swear I could have been a teacher; I would have loved to try the leather elbow patch and tweed look.

It was boarded up in February 2008, just after it had been 'vandalised'. I suspect it was that incident which prodded the 'owner' to cover it up before more damage transpired.

In spring 2008 this piece was on sale on eBay. It was first offered with a starting bid of $300,000, but received no bids, and was soon re-listed with a £120,000 start price.

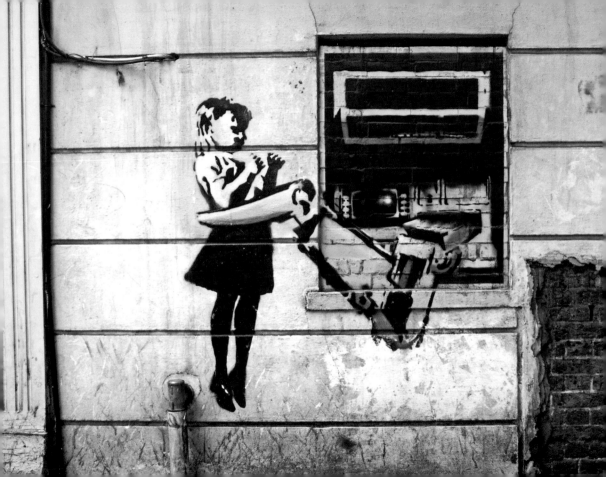

cash machine & girl - cont

The eBay description wrote, **"Due to planned building work we are pleased to offer this iconic 'cash machine girl' a well-documented original Banksy up for closed auction. The centre-piece is on a bricked-up window and will be removed as one piece, this and the rest of the work will involve conservation specialists in a controlled removal. The detached piece will be mounted on a new lightweight surface replicating the original wall and can therefore be presented free-standing or hanging when completed. The company that we strongly recommend to undertake this work have done this a number of times before with Banksy works of art... The cost of this work is put at around Ŀ29,000.00... The painting is in fair condition at the present time... there are localised areas of flaking paint, but in general the paint layers are stable. There are areas of recently applied white emulsion over parts of the painting, but tests indicate that this can be carefully dissolved and removed from the stencil painted surface without damage to Banksy's work. At present the painting is covered and boxed-in".**

Considering the piece is still on the wall, and still has the large strips of paint on it, I assume that nothing happened in response to this ambitiously feeble sales pitch.

Status

In mid October 2009 the piece was suddenly revealed again (not long after the shop next door changed its name to 'Banksy Bagel Bar'!), although it was now under some complicated plastic and wood protection. In June 2010 the 'shop' section on Banksy's web site showed a photo of the Bagel bar and sardonically commented that **"Banksy does not produce greeting cards or print photo-canvases or paint commissions or sell freshly baked bagels"**. The Bagel Shop had since been replaced by a Dry Cleaner; presumably a victim of the Great Global Bagel Depression of 2012.

The two large strips of paint are still there (October 2013) so presumably the owner of the wall hasn't tried to restore it. The photo opposite shows it in 2010, which is probably the only time my reflection will be in the same photo as Cheryl Cole, a Banksy, and a 'Banksy Bagel Bar'.

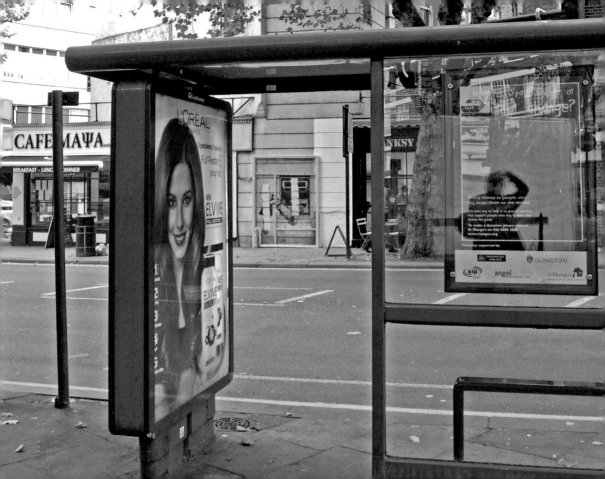

papa 'rat' d

This was on the entrance wall of the 'Movie World' shop, on Exmouth Market, from at least early 2004 (Post Code - EC1R 4QL. Map/GPS reference - TQ 31296 82489).

It was another good example of the mutant photographer-cum-rat and of how Banksy pieces are given a respect not afforded to most vandals, as during repainting they carefully kept the Banksy.

But it slowly peeled away over time and when I walked past in October 2009 the wall was totally white and the Banksy had gone. The shop had also changed to 'McCaul Goldsmiths'.

Rather more interestingly the building has an English Heritage blue plaque on it, which informs us that the famous clown Joseph Grimaldi lived there from 1818 to 1828.

Every year a memorial service is held for Grimaldi at the Holy Trinity Church in Dalston. Clowns from all over the world come in full clown clobber. Now that's what I call a church service worth going to! Some great photos are available at - www.ukstudentlife.com/Ideas/Album/ClownService.htm

A Clowns Museum/Exhibition exists at the Wookey Hole attraction in Somerset, so if you are visiting Banksy's 'This is not a Photo Opportunity' stencil in Cheddar Gorge (see BLT Vol 2 for full details), you can follow up the clown connection there. I bet my mother will be so proud of me; from budding writer to washed-up clown expert all in the space of a few cider soaked years.

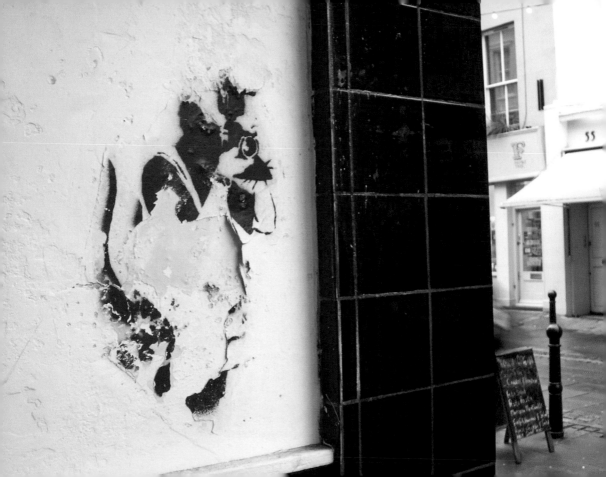

placard rat - 'always fail(e)'

Post Code - EC1R 3AS
Map / GPS reference - TQ 31011 82486

Location & Various Tittle-Tattle (and 'Team Robbo' again...)

By a bus stop on the Farringdon Road (A201), near the junction with Calthorpe Street.

This is another addition to the canon of Banksy placard rats. It's been there since at least mid 2005 and used to declare 'Always Fail', but was slightly amended in mid-2006 to read 'Always Faile', which may or may not have been a cheeky pun from the Faile crew.

'Always Fail' is also a nickname for the Royal Mail, whose massive Mount Pleasant sorting office can be seen in the background of the photo. I used to do some casual work there and it really is as grim as you would expect and the managers there really do always fail. The real workers are nice though and having things like yam and plantain in the canteen was a nice touch for the distinctly multi-cultural workforce.

In late February 2010 the placard was amended to read, in chunky black marker pen, 'Team Robbo!', presumably as part of the fallout from the now infamous 'Robbo' incident, when Banksy amended/went over a very old piece by veteran writer Robbo on the Regent's Canal in Camden, and all hell broke loose afterwards.

Since then various amendments have come and gone, and the original Banksy message is certainly never going to be seen again.

Status

Faded, but still there and looking excellent, despite regular DIY writing on the placard area (October 2013)

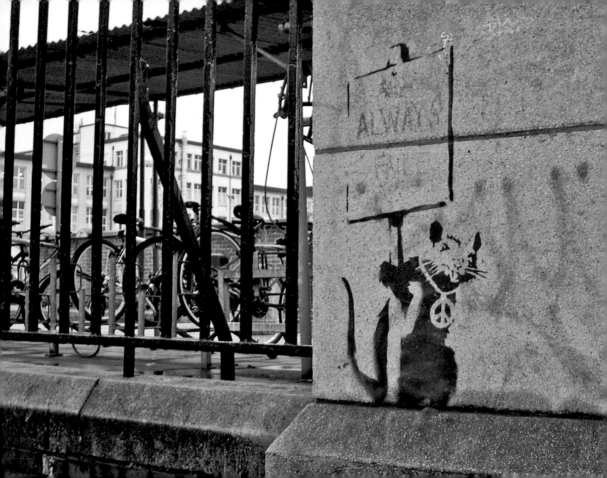

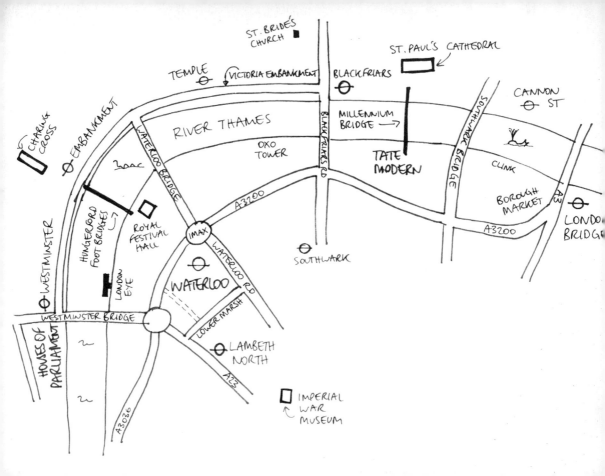

Waterloo, South Bank & Victoria Embankment

a.k.a. the riverside rat tour...

This tour went around the Lower Marsh / Waterloo station area, then all along the South Bank from the mortar rats (opposite the Houses of Parliament) to London Bridge, before crossing over the River Thames to visit the locations on the North side of the river, finishing at Embankment tube station. The route went close to lots of tourist attractions and in some ways was the most pleasant of the three tours.

The art featured on this tour was pretty much obliterated in the years after BLT was released. There is virtually nothing left now, so if you do seek out the few faded remains don't drag your other half along for the whole route as they might end up very unimpressed at your geekdom.

Or even worse, dragging your first date out and pointing at a bare wall, saying "That's where the 'Girl with Balloon' was... in 2005... (long pause followed by groan and blank look)... you know... it's your favourite Banksy... the one with... um... the heart shaped balloon... is she letting it go or trying to catch it? It's very deep you know".

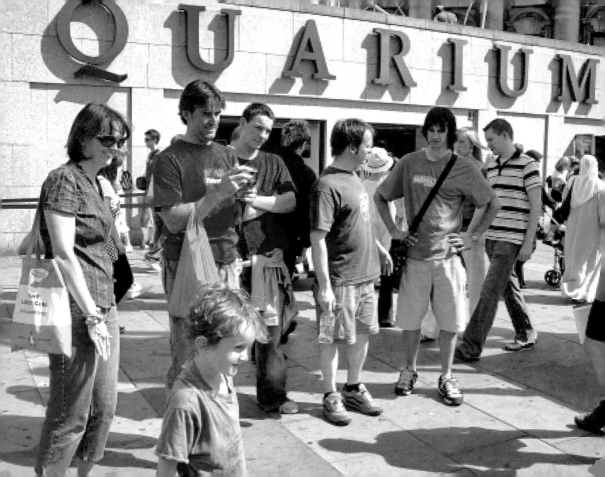

writing rat

This rat was on the corner of Lower Marsh and Baylis Road (Post Code - SE1 7AB. Map/GPS reference - TQ 31209 79751)

It seems like Banksy blitzed the Lower Marsh area at some point as this one, and the next three locations, were all dotted along this historic street.

This is a rat piece I've not seen elsewhere; with a marker pen in its hand.

It was on a metal telecoms box (always a favourite Banksy target) but had already been buffed even before the 1st edition of BLT struggled out from the printers in late 2006.

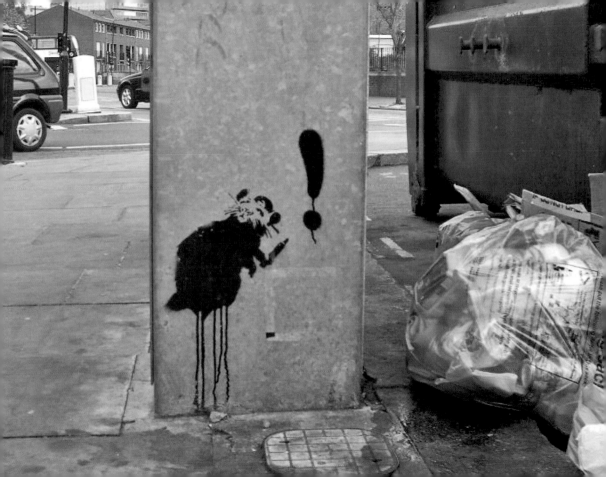

ghetto blaster rat

Previously on the metal delivery box outside 'Supreme General Stores' on Lower Marsh (Post Code - SE1 7AB. Map/GPS reference - TQ 31161 79762)

This used one of Banksy's favourite mediums; the metal boxes outside newsagents, and was often partly obscured by posters.

The entire metal box later vanished and was replaced by a nice new one. A man in the shop told me it had been stolen (in about early February 2007 I believe).

In April 2008 my wonderful mate Stef who did the original graphic design for this book, plus various flyers and publicity materials, and who smoked copious fags in typical arty mode, was wandering in Hong Kong (as you do...), during what was mainly a trip to the Philippines (as you have...) and came across a show of Banksy art, at the Schoeni Art Gallery. It included this rat, still on the metal newsagent delivery box. Considering that the man in the shop told me it had been stolen, I no longer know what to believe now.

Part of the exhibition was originally at the Hong Kong Arts Centre the week before, and was entitled 'Love Art', although publicity material liberally used the embarrassingly dire phrase 'Banksy robs Hong Kong' in big letters. It rather controversially seemed to suggest that Banksy was 'exhibiting' there, whereas I would think it's safe to assume he hadn't touched it with the proverbial pooey stick.

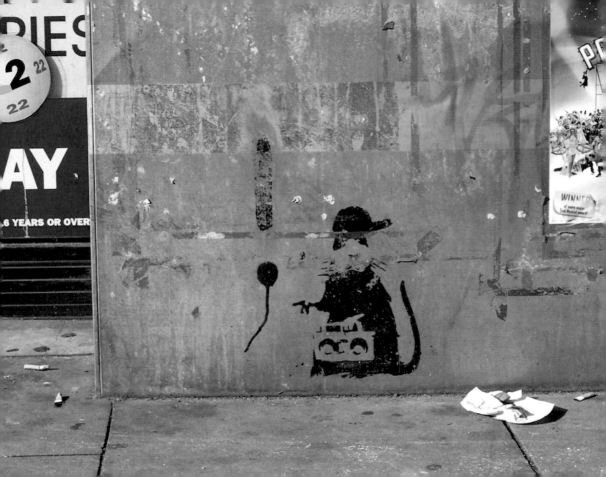

designated picnic area

Previously on the side of a skanky alley about half way along Lower Marsh, next to what used to be 'Crockatt & Powell Booksellers' (Post Code - SE1 7AD. Map/GPS reference - TQ 31070 79688)

This had been there since at least mid 2004 and the arrow invariably pointed to a pile of binbags or rotting veg, as Lower Marsh is still a very active and historic market area.

It was pretty much buffed by the local Council in late 2006 (see inset photo) even though the bookshop owners didn't want it removed and had told them that. They had therefore gone against the 'laws' of graffiti removal, although I always find it rather absurd that there are 'laws' on removing so-called vandalism.

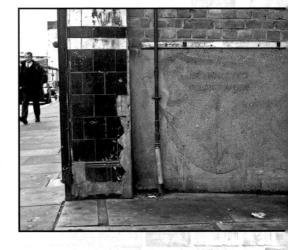

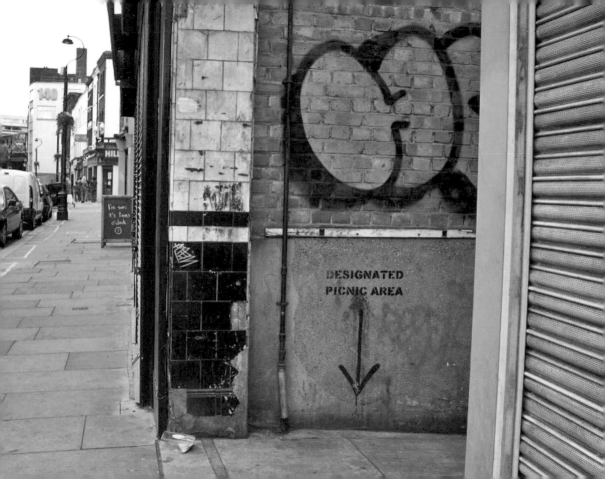

help me rat

Formerly on the metal delivery box outside a newsagent on Lower Marsh (Post Code - SE1 7AE. Map/GPS reference - TQ 31017 79637)

This rat scrawling 'help me' was not one I'd seen elsewhere.

It had been happily sitting untouched on a newsagent's metal box since at least mid 2005, but in early 2007 the 'help me' phrase was defaced (see inset photo). By mid March the whole box had gone and the shop always seemed to be closed.

Later I was emailled out of the blue by the new 'owner' who said that he bought the box from the newsagent before it closed down.

In April 2009 it appeared in an art auction, by an auction house that should not only know better, but also doesn't deserve the valuable publicity I might accidentally give them.

Four of the five street pieces in the auction failed to sell, and the fifth (this one), was withdrawn before the auction.

This unfortunately was later being touted for sale by Bankrobber Gallery (see F8 above for a similar story). I was surprised though at the photo of it on their web site because last time I photographed it on the street the 'help me' writing had clearly been dogged.

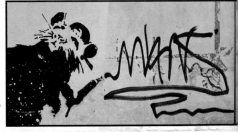

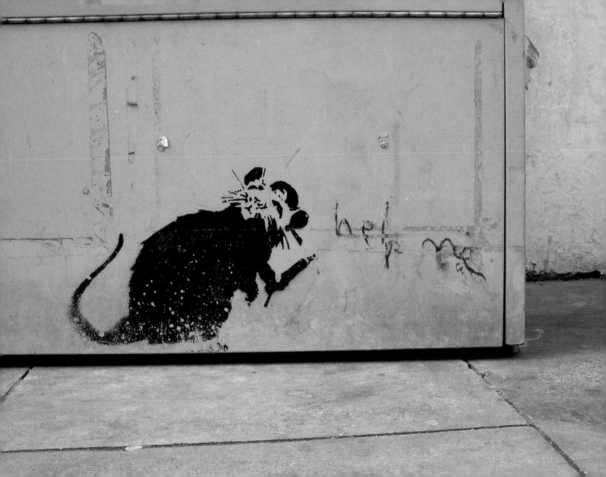

monkey detonator

This was in the tunnel underneath Waterloo Train Station, which is also known as Leake Street (Post Code - SE1 7AE. Map/GPS reference - TQ 30997 79717).

When I took a group on a free tour of art/graffiti in Shoreditch in 2006, one observation I heard was that they'd "never been in so many skanky alleys in my life". This scabby underpass beneath Waterloo train station was far more wee stained skanky, and was the perfect place for a monkey to detonate a bunch of bananas. A photo of it is featured in the 'Wall and Piece' book, which dates it to 2003, and it has also been shown on Mr.B's web site.

It was grey washed in October 2006 (see inset photo) and once the press heard about it many months later, and printed the seemingly obligatory half true story, there were a few transport bosses left with egg on their faces at painting over 'a Banksy'.

This tunnel later became famous for hosting The Cans Festival, a free event that took place on the May Bank Holiday weekend in 2008 (see BLT Vol 2 for full details and plenty of photos). Banksy (and many other artists) did loads of stencil based work in the tunnel, and the public were invited to queue up and look at it. About 28,500 people did so.

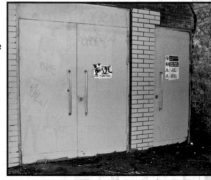

The tunnel was later refreshed by traditional graffiti writers, and in February 2010 it was also the site for the pop-up cinema that premiered his film 'Exit Through the Gift Shop'.

An early version of this image was used years previously in Bristol. It was smaller, had a shorter cord, and the explosive was traditional sticks of dynamite. A canvas of that version was sold at the Severnshed exhibition (Bristol) in early 2000.

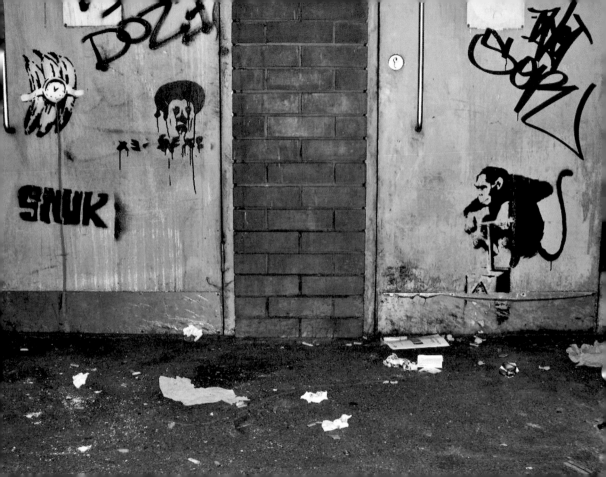

snorting copper

Banksy's infamous Snorting Copper used to sniff just outside the tunnel underneath Waterloo Station (Leake Street - Post Code - SE1 7NN. Map/GPS reference - TQ 30890 79791)

It was partly shown in 'Wall and Piece', which dates it to 2005. The book mixes and matches photos of this copper with the whiteline from the one that existed in Shoreditch (see location S19).

By the time of the Cans Festival in May 2008 (see location R5 on the previous page for details) it still just about remained. But it got surrounded by other art, and was constantly photographed by people who seemed to think it had been done especially for the festival.

The whole wall was surprisingly blackwashed in September 2008, thus totally wiping out the copper. I write surprisingly because it was this wall which stated that the festival site was maintained by 'blank expression', the company that helped get permission for the festival, and which said it administered 'legal' areas / walls that people had donated for art use. I can't find any trace of it now though.

Note the lovely Space Invader that used to be above it (see inset photo).

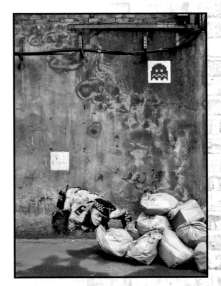

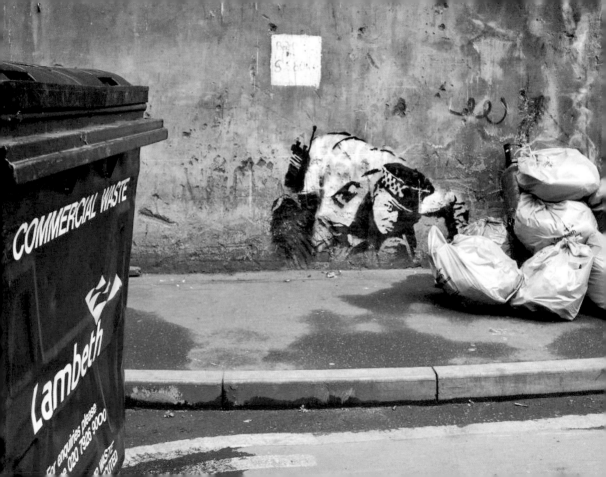

R7

mortar rats

Two separate (but similar) examples of these rats existed on the granite blocks of the riverside pedestrianised walk of the South Bank from about 2003. One (see main photo) was close to Westminster Bridge (Post Code - SE1 7EH. Map/GPS reference - TQ 30575 79516). The other was several hundred metres further West, towards Lambeth Bridge (inset photo).

The Houses of Parliament and 'Big Ben' can just be spotted, looming in the background; the rats assumed 'target' (see inset photo for possible trajectory).

The one on my main photo is shown in Banksy's little 'Existencilism' book, next to a comment that "Rats are called rats because they'll do anything to survive". It was also used on his web site.

Banksy's tag was just visible in the corner of each. One had some diving figures added to it (the inset photo version). I've always assumed they were not by Banksy as they spoil the composition.

Despite being untouched for many years, both were buffed in mid-2007.

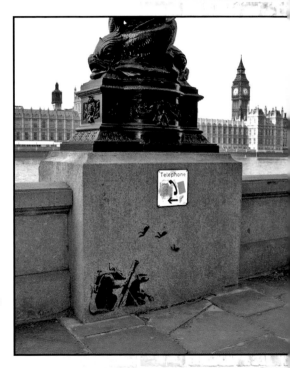

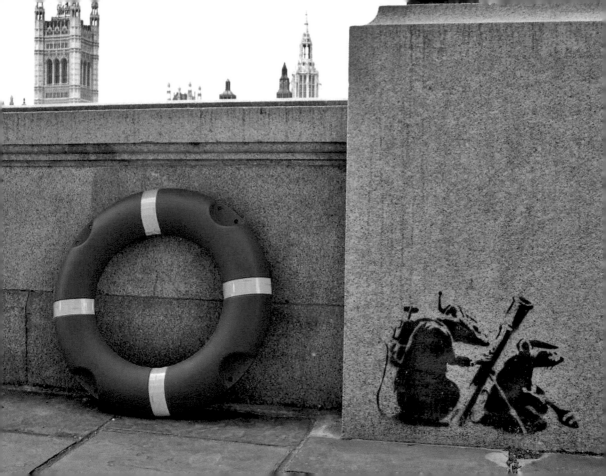

this is not a photo opportunity

This was on the granite blocks of the pedestrianised riverside walk of the South Bank, close to the London Eye from at least early 2003 (Post Code - SE1 7JA. Map/GPS reference - TQ 30594 79812).

This was possibly Banksy's most photographed stencil, as many people deliberately or accidentally got their photos taken here because it overlooks the Houses of Parliament. Photos of tourists looking dumb next to it are included in both his 'Wall and Piece' and 'Existencilism' books.

It was surprisingly buffed in mid February 2007. I write 'surprisingly' because it had been there about four years, in a very high profile place, so it seemed a bit random that it was buffed then, rather than anytime previously.

This stencil is his most travelled, and has been used in Glasgow, Cuba (Habana), France (used twice in the same area - both placed so they could be photographed with the Eiffel Tower in the background), and Australia (ditto, but using the Sydney Opera House). It was also used twice more along the South Bank (see locations R11 & R12), as well as in the Swiss Embassy car park in London, and on a rock face in Cheddar Gorge, Somerset. See BLT Vol 2 for both of those locations, which still exist to this day.

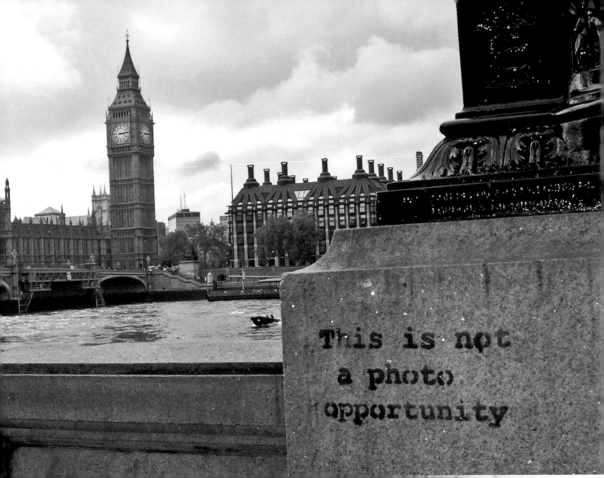

BLT TIP

This area (R7 to R9) is a good vicinity to spot the white line on the South Bank walkway.

This was a white line that stretched for a long way. It seems to start around the London Eye area, and runs along the South Bank, over Lambeth Road and around the houses to a bridge in Whitgift Street. I thought a snorting copper was supposed to be at that end but I've never seen a photo of it and no evidence of it could be seen when I first 'walked the line' in 2006.

The line was partly shown in 'Wall and Piece', which dates it to 2005. The book mixes and matches photos of this whiteline and the one that existed in Shoreditch (see location S19). It also shows the Snorting Copper from near Waterloo station (location R6) as if the white line (or another line?) was supposed to go there.

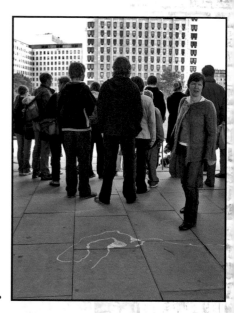

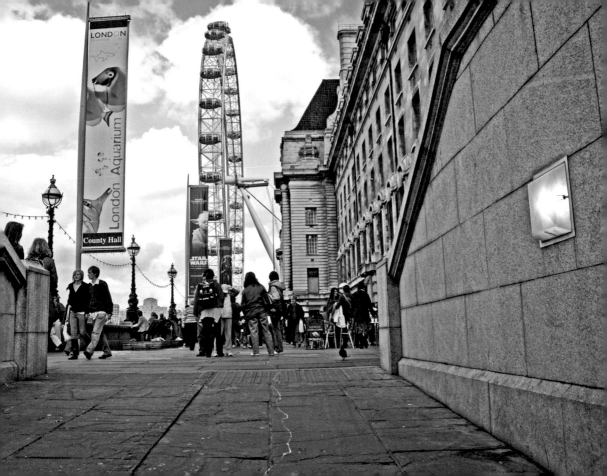

sawing rat

This rare sawing rat, complete with cigarette and beret, was on the granite blocks of the South Bank pedestrianised walk from at least 2003, just before the Hungerford Footbridges (Post Code - SE1 7NN. Map/GPS reference - TQ 30890 79791).

The circle on the pavement that accompanied these sawing rats had already gone before I took this photograph.

It deteriorated more during its lifetime and was fully buffed in mid 2007.

BLT TIP

There were two Girl With Balloon stencils along the South Bank.

Both have gone, but are still slightly visible as ghostly shapes.

One was on the East side of Waterloo Bridge (by the National Theatre). The other was on the East side of Blackfriars Bridge.

There were also a few 'Buried Treasure' stencils along the riverside walk but they have also virtually gone.

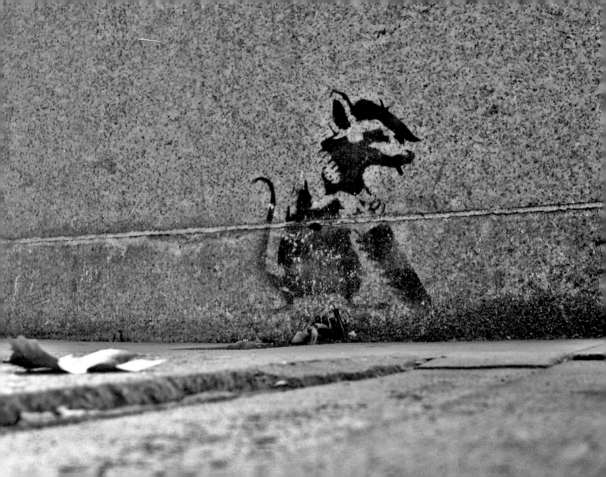

ghetto blaster rat

This was also on the granite blocks of the riverside walk along the South Bank, by the entrance to Festival Pier (Post Code - SE1 8XZ - Map/GPS reference - TQ 30764 80331)

It has been there since at least spring 2004 and can still vaguely be seen, but it has previously been scrawled over with some bubble graffiti, which was then roughly removed, meaning the rat is now so faded that it's hardly worth a visit.

BLT TIP

'BORING' was infamously sprayed by Banksy in massive red letters on the Waterloo Bridge side of the National Theatre.

He used a modified fire extinguisher to achieve it.

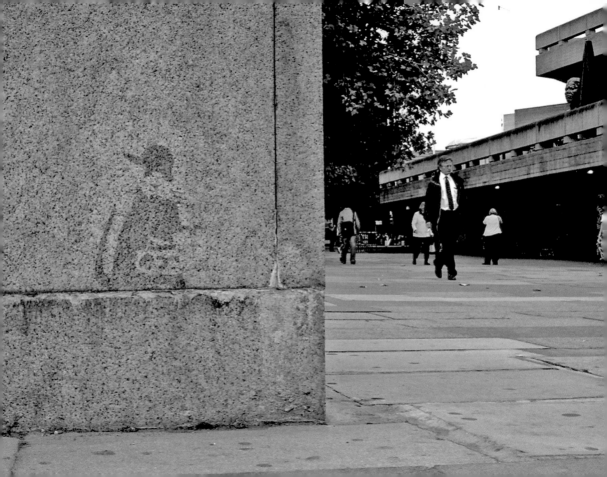

this is not a photo opportunity

This was on a rusting old rubbish bin, on the pedestrianised walkway of the South Bank, right outside the Tate Modern (Post Code - SE1 9TG. Map/GPS reference - TQ 31973 80541).

It had been there since at least mid 2002 (when the bin looked far more salubrious), but the bin slowly rusted away until it was painted afresh in mid 2007.

Note the amateur Banksy 'homage' also in the photo, dating from 2004. It's of a tiny weeing soldier (a classic older Banksy piece), and is tagged as 'spank me', using the typeface ('stop') that Banksy used to use for his tag.

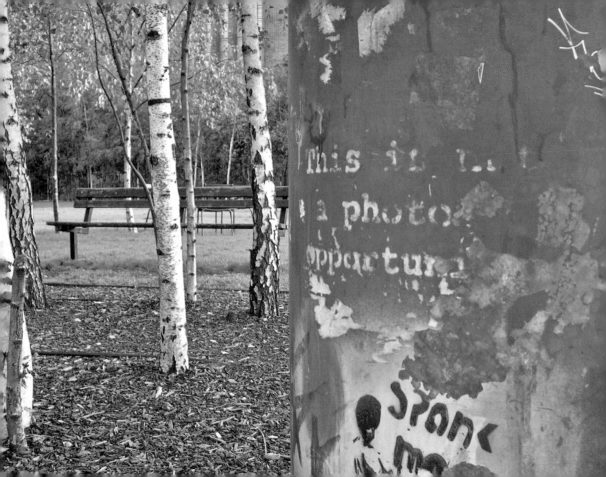

this is not a photo opportunity

This was rather famously on a lovely old building on Park Street, behind Borough Market (Post Code - SE1 9TG. Map / GPS reference - TQ 31973 80541).

It was sprayed around 2003 and I was always surprised how long it lasted considering how historic and well known the building is.

The location was used as the hideaway in the 1998 film 'Lock Stock and Two Smoking Barrels', and I've also spotted several magazine photo shoots that used this setting and the stencil (before it was buffed). Maybe irony is lost on the latter?

In an outrageous bit of spot jockeying a black stencilled 'flying box' was added right above the Banksy in mid 2007 (see photo - by the by, is it just me or are those man's shoes too big for his body? Discuss amongst yourselves for a minute whilst I get back on track with the art research). It was by a South African artist called 'straat-toe' which translates from Afrikaans as 'to the streets'.

Both were heavily sandblasted off in January 2008.

In October 2011 someone did a rather poor copy of an old Banksy stencil (the 'Laugh Now' monkey) in the exact place where the 'photo op' was. Another was done just around the street corner.

BLT TIP

As you walk past the 'London Bridge Tandoori Restaurant' on the south side of London Bridge (Post Code - SE1 9QG / Map/GPS reference- TQ 32701 80267), you might recognise the advertising hoarding where Banksy scrawled 'The Joy of Not Being Sold Anything'.

The making of this slogan was shown years ago in a video on Mr.B's web site, and a still shot is used in the 'Pictures of Walls' book.

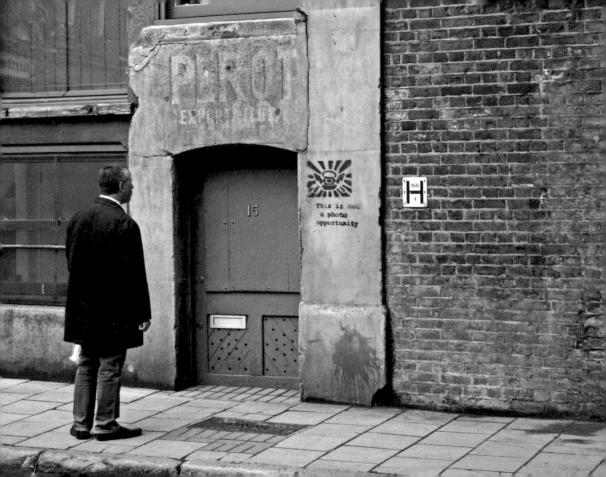

R13

placard rat - "you lose"

Post Code - EC4R 3UE
Map / GPS reference - TQ 32586 80661

Location & The Bit Where I Get All Serious (for once)

At the riverside end of All Hallow's Lane, which means it is well-nigh directly underneath Cannon Street station.

A glimpse of this street piece was briefly featured in Banksy's excellent film 'Exit Through the Gift Shop'.

Of all the placard rats this one always sticks in my mind because when I first visited it I found a guy next to it, living in a cardboard box, with little except a radio and a blanket. It felt really meaningless to take photos of it, and it could also have been demeaning to him. So I talked with him for a long time, asked 'permission' to take a photo of the wall, and I consciously decided not to include him in the photo.

The aptness of the placard message dug home.

This is just one reason I support The Big Issue, try to talk to people I meet rather than just walk on by, and try to help them a little. I don't always succeed in doing this, so I need hefty reminders sometimes.

Status

It's been there since at least mid 2005, and although it has faded a lot in the last few years, it is still visible (October 2013). It even valiantly survived the tunnel being redeveloped twice, in 2007/8, and 2011.

BLT TIP

It is difficult to explain how to get to R14 from here. A map and the use of the subways at Blackfriars station will help.

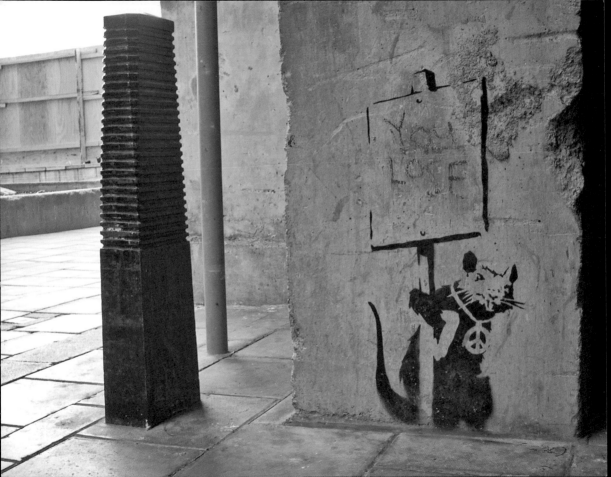

poison rat

Post Code - EC4Y 8AU
Map / GPS reference - TQ 31573 81134

Location & Stuff About Architecture & Green Waste (that isn't Friday night sick)

Just off Bride Lane.

This has been on the steps of a little passageway to St. Bride's Church since at least late 2005.

Although this has never been the greatest Poison Rat in London, I always think it is the one with the best setting, as it not only has St. Bride's Church (the historic 'Fleet Street' church with its stunning 'wedding cake' style spire) and the achingly gorgeous Lutyens designed Reuters Building (a.k.a. 85 Fleet Street) hogging the backdrop, but it also cleverly uses the steps as if the rat is pouring the toxic waste down them.

Status

Very faded but still there (October 2013). The green waste is no longer perceptible though.

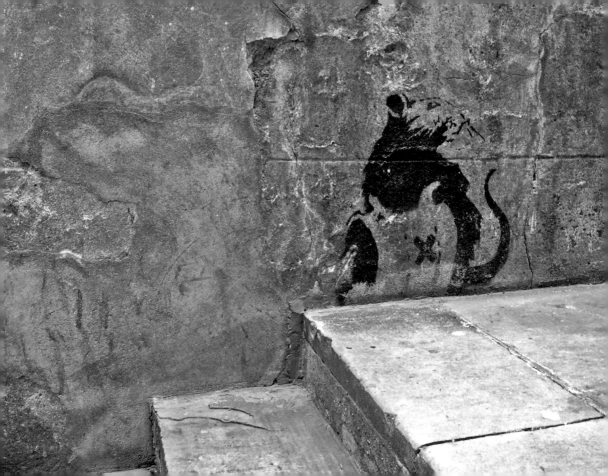

photographer rat

Previously on a metal utilities box on the pavement of the Victoria Embankment (A3211) near the boat HMS President (Post Code - EC4Y 0HJ. Map/GPS reference - TQ 31320 80802).

This Banksy stencil seemed to get given respect by many others. Each time I saw it, since early 2005, it had a different variety of stickers surrounding it, but they were always around it rather than directly on top of it.

In late 2008 it seems as though the box was removed, and replaced by a different one. That seems slightly strange eh? How did they manage that without sanctioned connivance?

In January 2009 the box was offered for sale on 'Gumtree', the popular Aussie / Kiwi / Saffa / Hippie layabout web site, and it had apparently been on eBay before; although I didn't see that. The cheeky monkey even referenced my book as some sort of provenance (see the 'Buy Bye Bye, Sale Sell Sell' part at the start of this book for a rant about people who do that). Being in my book doesn't mean it is by Banksy. Only he can positively confirm or deny that; and he will not. So there is no legitimate provenance for street pieces, and quite right too.

In April 2009 it then appeared in an art auction, by an auction house that should not only know better, but also doesn't deserve the publicity I might accidentally give them. I want to give information about these pieces, but I don't want in anyway to help these people to try to sell pieces that were created for the streets (not for auction houses, trendy bars or living rooms). It had an estimate of £12,000-18,000 attached to it, plus the dreaded 'Vermin Certificate of Authenticity'. They said it had been 'salvaged' from a 'decommissioned telephone exchange box'. At this point I felt like screaming. People used to actually work for a living, and produce things. Now they just rent out property, become politicians, or try to sell ripped off street art.

Four of the five street pieces in this ill-advised auction failed to sell (including this one), and the fifth was withdrawn before the auction.

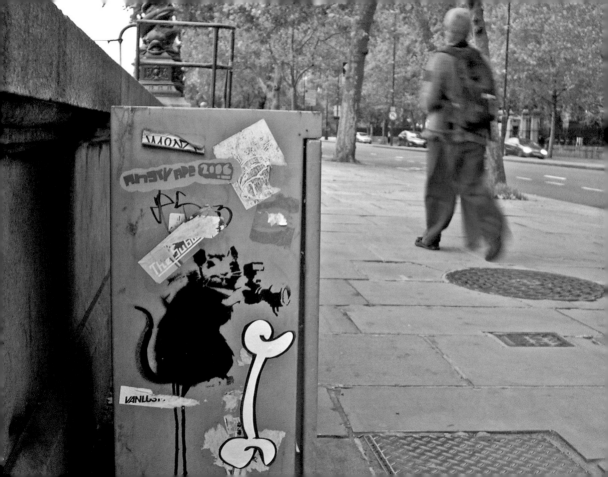

placard rat + question mark

Post Code - WC2R 2PP
Map/GPS reference - TQ 31043 80786

Location & Hopeless Attempts At Small Talk (I am a man after all)

On the granite blocks of the riverside wall, near a memorial on the Victoria Embankment (A3211). Right next to where the boat HQS Wellington is moored. Opposite Temple tube station.

Is that enough location info for you?

An excellent rat, with a big question mark on the placard. It's definitely been there since February 2005, but probably actually dates from around 2003.

A small photo rat used to exist on the Temple Place side of Temple tube station (opposite Arundel Street), but it went quite a while ago. This morsel of history proves though that this locale has had a lot of Banksy activity in the past.

Status

Still vaguely visible (October 2013) but very faded and a bad buff job I assume.

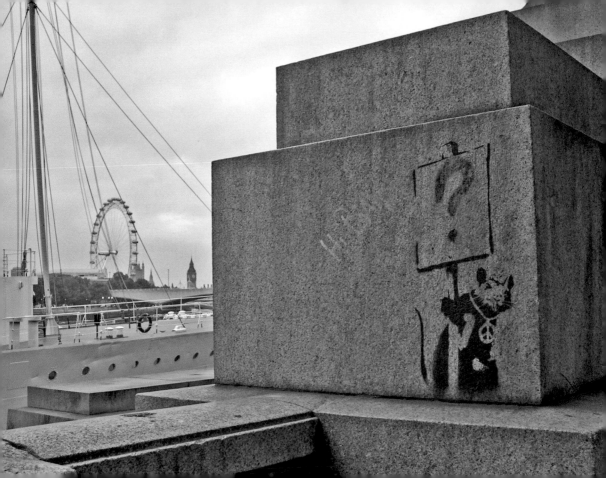

photographer rat

This was above a green utilities box under Waterloo Bridge (the corner with Savoy Street), until it was buffed in mid 2007 (Post Code - **EC4Y 0HJ**. Map/GPS reference - **TQ 31320 80802**).

That's me that is. A photographer rat.

This was a very clean rat until rude, and frankly rather confused, graffiti was added close to it. Something about polos, Banksy and an unnatural act.

Note the 'Cept' tag on the utilities box - a rare sight this far south.

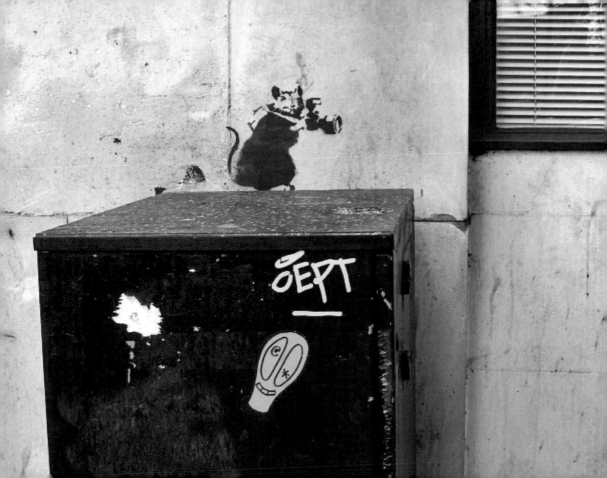

placard rat -
'go back to bed'

Previously on the East side of the massive concrete
struts of the Hungerford footbridge, opposite
Embankment tube station (Post Code - WC2N 6NS.
Map/GPS reference - TQ 30438 80323).

This was another of the popular 'Go Back To Bed' rats,
faithfully spreading the gospel since at least mid 2004.
It was perfectly placed to catch commuters and early
morning joggers, both of whom really should have
known better.

It was buffed in mid 2006, even before the 1st edition
of this book could actually see the light of day.

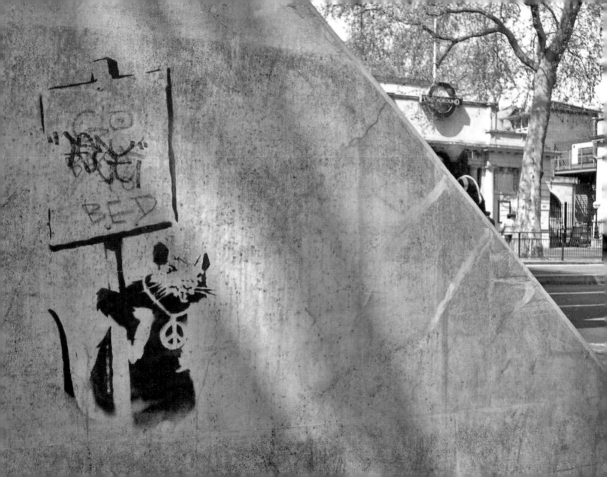

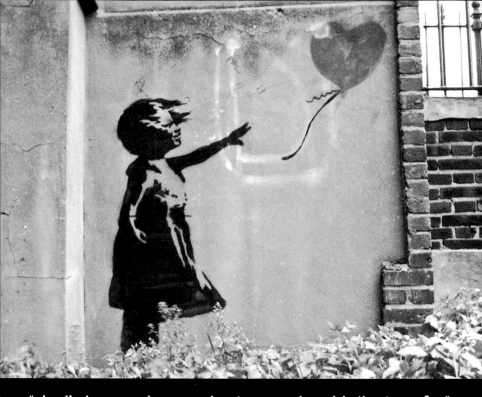

"when the time comes to leave, just walk away quietly and don't make any fuss"

Le Fin

THANKS & ACKNOWLEDGEMENTS

Obviously the real credit must go to Banksy, and all the writers / artists who do their work for free on the street. Without them publishers would have nothing to show readers! Please support them. Details of some websites are on the following pages.

My first, and biggest thanks is for the wonderful Stef who started this whole crazy thing off in 2006 by asking me, in one of those fuzzy Friday afternoon moments, if I had ever thought of making my free tours, info and photos into anything more, such as a book? I had - great minds thinks alike eh - but the locations book mapped out in my head was mainly about Eine's shop shutters, rather than Banksy. That's how BLT started, on the back of the proverbial bar napkin. He then pushed me all the way through the process, and after a lot of hard work BLT arrived, and was updated regularly over the next few years. Stef did all of the painstaking graphic design for the first 3 editions (plus the print preparation, flyers and anything I needed!) and the cover of the 4th edition. What a mug! But seriously, I'm genuinely not sure if any of this would have ever got started without him and I therefore owe him much love.

My second thanks has to be for Sam, who has handled all the print brokerage on my books, helped me on the streets in the earlier days, generally encouraged me, and was always around for a chat and a wander. His soul brother Dave has also provided a similar vital service in the later years.

General respect to Steve at 'Art of the State' and Tristan Manco, godfathers of art and graffiti info, knowledge and photographs.

And as mentioned at the start of the book, thanks to all the people who responded to my leading questions and annoyance of where to find some of this art, or who even accidentally gave some info. Particular mention must be given to anyone who contributes to flickr, especially the Banksy group, and above all my fellow volunteers at the Banksy group; Jason, Ian, Mel, Quel and Steve (again).

Although this book is in no way sanctioned by Pictures On Walls or The Big Issue, I greatly respect them both and give thanks for their existence. Particular thanks to lovely Steph who used to manage POW.

CREDITS

All text and photographs (bar three photos listed below) in this book are by me, Martin Bull. Hand printed, limited editions of my black and white film photos of art from the streets are sometimes available via 'shellshockphotos' on eBay or www.shellshockpublishing.co.uk, depending on whether I have dark room facilities at the time and / or can pull my finger out.

* Many thanks to Dave and Juliette for their photograph of the Shoreditch tour in September 2006 (shown just before location S18)

* Many thanks to Sam for his photograph of the Waterloo/South Bank tour in August 2006 (shown at the introduction to that section)

* Many thanks to Karen Richardson for her photograph of the Bomb Hugger at Fabric (location F6)

Many, many thanks again to Stef at Hoodacious - www.hoodacious.co.uk - for the graphic design and print preparation of the first 3 editions of this book and also help with the 4th edition.

some relevant web sites/shout outs guaranteed to improve our miserable lives

Banksy – www.banksy.co.uk
Pictures On Walls (POW) – www.picturesonwalls.com

Faile – www.faile.net
Arofish – www.arofish.org.uk
Space Invader – www.space-invaders.com
Obey Giant (Shepard Fairey) – www.obeygiant.com
Blek Le Rat – http://bleklerat.free.fr/ & http://blekmyvibe.free.fr
Cept – www.spradio.com
Eine – www.einesigns.co.uk
Before Chrome / Burning Candy – http://theburningcandy.blogspot.com
Mantis – www.themantisproject.co.uk

Art of the State – www.artofthestate.co.uk
The Mighty Gas – www.bristolrovers.co.uk
Graffoto blog – www.graffoto.co.uk
TU ink – www.tuink.co.uk
The Big Issue – www.bigissue.co.uk
Hoodacious – www.hoodacious.co.uk
The Banksy group on flickr – www.flickr.com/groups/banksy
PM Press – www.pmpress.org
My own website – www.shellshockpublishing.co.uk

STILL AVAILABLE - BLT VOL. 2

This unique, unofficial, and unashamedly DIY book follows on from BLT1 by rounding up the rest of Banksy's UK graffiti from 2006 to 2010, as well as older survivors. It includes over 135 different locations of Banksy's street pieces, past and present (almost half of which are still worth visiting); information, random facts & idle chit-chat on each location; a full walking tour of his remaining work in Bristol; and also snippets of art/graffiti by Eine, Faile, Inkie, Kato, Mode 2, BA / DBZ, and Rowdy.

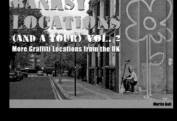

★   382 pages / With over 230 colour photos

★   1st Edition (Dec 2010) / ISBN: 978-0955471230

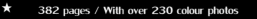

"...an eminently likeable book, full of down-to-earth humour and unexpected trivia.""
Venue Magazine - February 2011

"...a reminder of how far the nation's favourite tagger has come [and] an exhaustive guide to those subversive stencils and where to find them, with more than 200 photos and even a walking tour of Banksy pieces in his native Bristol."
Telegraph - January 2011

"Ellsworth-Jones writes perceptively about the 'ethical dilemmas' created by Banksy's marketing techniques, yet still communicates the excitement of a 'treasure hunt' for traces of his work in the scruffier purlieus of London" (*The Observer*)"
Review of someone else's book, whose aforementioned treasure hunt unashamedly uses my books to fill a whole chapter!

"This is an all new, completely different book [to Volume 1] featuring work not included in the previous offering. It's thick [and] ... a bit of a bargain price too with some of the proceeds going to charity."
www.artofthestate.co.uk

"This prosaic approach is refreshing in a book about street-art ... So, keen Banksy fan or merely mildly curious, this book delivers exactly what it promises: "...at the end of the day it's just a grown man doing what he enjoys in life" "
Eye Magazine - January 2011

WHAT'S BEEN SAID ABOUT BLT VOL.1

"BLT (Banksy Locations and Tours) is the new (unofficial) Banksy graffiti locations book, painstakingly compiled by Martin Bull.... I think Martin must have been a train spotter in a previous life – there's postcodes and GPS references for every location along with comments about the history of the piece or the things that have happened (hippies and strippers) when his tours have arrived at a site. It's pretty much Banksy all the way but he does include some other artists such as Eine, D face and Blek Le Rat. It's a great little book, kind of reminds me of the little Banksy books (but a lot thicker). Ideal for reading in the smallest room in the house."

   www.artofthestate.co.uk

5 stars out of 5
"Are you a big fan of Banksy and got no plans this summer? Then this is the perfect book for you. A no-nonsense travel guide to all his London locations."

   Bookseller review by Lee Thompson, Waterstone's Sheffield Orchard branch

"Don't buy this book, it's a little bit too much Banksy..."

   Review on You Tube by 'yourARTescortFRANKLY'

Guardian art critic, Jonathan Jones, did an article on Banksy on 5 July 2007. The article, entitled 'Best of British?' included the following section.... "Perhaps the jokes are funnier, the images more emotional when you encounter them in the streets. Yet as I test that proposition, something rapidly makes me hold my guidebook to Banky's (sic) street art – that's right, there's a guidebook, Martin Bull's Banksy Locations and Tours – under tables in coffee shops, or skulk in alleys while reading it, in case anyone notices I'm actually seeking out this stuff."

   www.guardian.co.uk

"This is the fantastic Banksy: Locations & Tours book that has become a cult favourite in the street art world. It is an ideal companion for anybody visiting London to see Banksy pieces in the flesh... don't waste time researching and printing maps. Grab this book & do it in one easy step. This book has sold out virtually everywhere, so this is an ideal opportunity to buy a slice of Banksy history."

   eBay seller who seems to have taken his sales pitch rather too far!

Brand New Unwanted Gift. Great Book.... Start off (bidding) at 99p.

   a different eBay seller (this made I larf! ☺)